In the beginning God created the heaven and earth.

Earth was void, formless, and was covered with deep darkness.

God's spirit was moving on waters…

Evening darkness had sunken on the city. Feeling exhaustion of the day all over his body, he was moving slowly in city streets with a computer in his hand. Shop fronts were gleaming glitteringly as if they were celebrating the approaching new year. Entire city was preparing for Christmas. Ever since childhood, the radiant lights of the shop windows and the approaching new year had always elated him. Snow on the city that day just before Christmas was giving him a taste of fable. He was inching along the avenues of this massive city while watching the brilliant shops and dressed Noel trees. Now he was on the busy street which he considered the prettiest in the entire city. New York... the city of his dreams...

Nicholas was born in a small town. He had a happy and peaceful childhood with his siblings, parents and friendly, warm residents of the town. He recalled dreaming of this city always after lying in his bed, exhausted in the evenings upon return from day's games played in that little town. His dream was to be a successful businessman in New York City. He started work immediately after graduation, job life and day to day events, time had passed.

His dream became reality and he got what he wanted. At age thirty-three he had a successful career and a good life in New York...

Still, he carried in his heart always not only a joy, but also a hope sprinkled with question marks. An insistent, continuously self-reminding dream recurring even when he has forgotten, which has settled nearly at the center of his life and he could not resolve, and one that has changed his life since age seventeen...

This dream, unanswered questions in his mind, he continued walking while noticing the shining shops at the road-side. He enjoyed walking home in the evenings after work. He was as if mesmerized while walking. Although the distance between his work and home was quite long he always preferred walking. It was as if his dreams accompanied him during these walks. He thought over his problems, questioned life and perhaps achieved some inner-peace, but most importantly he considered what his recurring dream meant.

Occasionally along the way he repeated the sentence "One day some things will happen, one day the secret of this dream will be revealed".

Through its frequent recurrence, the dream which he disregarded initially changed his life later involuntarily. While passing the sparkling streets, he was thinking of transformations he experienced due to the dream. In those days he had changed so suddenly that this was noticed not only by his parents, but also by the peaceful residents of that sweet town where he lived. It was as if the old mischievous Nicholas the Menace was replaced with a smart young man who always spent time with the church priest, asking questions, reading the Bible and a variety of books. After school he mostly went to church and questioned the priest. Priest was very pleased of his visits, answered his questions patiently and gave him books as gifts. He had mentioned his dream to the priest. The priest had said "Nicholas, this is a magnificent dream... I am sure that person is a saint and will absolutely give you a sign".

He was jerked with the siren of an ambulance passing through. Memories remembered left a pleasant smile on his face. It was more than an hour since he left work. He was still walking and contemplating. He was fairly tired when he reached home. The day had gone by busy and running around. Prepared himself a feast in the kitchen. He chose to dine alone watching television. Preferring to be alone some days, he was distancing himself from everyone and trying to solve the secret occupying his mind. It was one of those days.

He finished dinner while watching the magnificent scenery from his terrace. Then, as if wanting to solve the questions relating to his dream, he sat at his computer. He was entering words at the Internet search engine and was examining the given pages one by one. He flipped through his books in which he noted for years. A while later, he left his desk. With the sadness of not having found again what he was looking for, he sat at the couch in front of the window. Took a book from his table, began reading. "The Secret"... The greatest best- seller phenomenon of recent times. He was reading this book for the third time. There were things in the book which just didn't fit. He had purchased this book hoping that it might have relevance to his dream.

He eyed the cover of the book. His thoughts on the book were unchanged. He was always mentioning these thoughts to his friends. He had even written them on this subject in his social media page. He entered his own page at the Facebook and started reading his writing titled "The Secret"...

"Print and visual media were used in the marketing of *The Secret*. A good advertisement campaign together with online videos introducing *The Secret*, and thus the result.

Lacking the knowledge of cosmos behind the symbology in religious teachings, and its interaction with mind, body and spirit; humanity has immersed itself without questioning in teachings, even if these are contrary to the religious culture, claiming to hold the truth.

I fear people's beliefs in religion and God will become chaotic through such books which begin with correct information but conclude with misleading results.

For this they also used the newest and most magnificent Quantum. Quantum physics is so fantastic and incredible... Yes, quantum physics will create the new century. But its comprehension is equally difficult and confusing. In reality, the most striking, even the most important thing for me about the quantum physics is the parallel universes...

The way quantum physics works is entirely different than the reason, result and logic relationship of the world in which we live. It works in a system, the rules of which force a person to understand, and awe as one comprehends them.

For example: according to information obtained from quantum physics exploring the depths of matter:

Everything is energy and everything we call non-living, even consider non-existing, has energy and exists just because we think of them and attribute energy to them... Moreover, these energies are so intertwined that none is a separate energy mold but all is an integrated whole including the observer.

In other words, when you look around, you will see your couch, carpet and a book standing apart and as separate items. But according to the quantum physics, the couch, carpet and the book vibrate at different frequencies and have a living consciousness appearing as a singular intertwined energy form.

Our thoughts not visible as matters are also wave lengths possessing their own frequencies and energy.

Quantum physics views all matter perceived separately as a continually vibrating, live, rhythmic patterned, mutually interacting, changing and transforming energy package.

Anyway, here I just wanted to explain a small portion from the workings of the Quantum described in *The Secret* for familiarization and in proportion to my perception capacity.

If our people were not to dive at each secret external information arriving and were to look at their religion, culture unbenownst to them and know how to research, then they would see that this secret exists in the operative system of a **PRAYER**.

And, they will see that this secret incomplete information being imposed on us with errors in the 21st Century has existed for centuries. If they once held the holy book, they would see...

In the holy book, the power of prayer and intend has been emphasized as being capable of influencing one's fate and even changing it. We see that prayer has been bestowed to us as a power by the Creator.

After meeting the physical and spiritual requirements, we leave the decision to the Creator in awareness of the reality that he knows best. And we also know that we can only possess things within the permission of the Creator.

<u>The error in *The Secret* and other similar books is that they attach the entire secret to the law of attraction in the thought world and project each of us as a small god.</u>

What I am trying to say is that they are combining mystical information of the East, sprinkling quantum on it and selling it to the humanity, to our uninformed people in search of the truth, as the recipe of the secret.

Although it is partially correct when it mentions a real operating mechanism as the point of origin for our thoughts, the sale of this mechanism as the "absolute power" is absolutely wrong. Because in reality, what this teaching is describing are the prayers. The book only omits the body language during a prayer and praying to the Creator. All it speaks of is the universe...

And this information carries the possibility of ruining the beliefs of uninformed people lacking religious precepts who only wish to learn the mechanism of attraction.

For this reason I say beware...

Let me also ask you: Have you been able to draw what you desire into your lives? You purchased and read the book in question. You applied the rules and everything verbatim. Have you been able to attract cheques with multiple zeros? Do you have a Ferrari at the front of your houses? What happened to getting rich and having Ferraris? Those who have succeeded- please drop a comment below... And those of us who haven't, do you really believe that it's not the fault of the system, but ours? Others have used the system and become rich, right? So we're the ones at fault, right? We couldn't affirm and focus correctly and couldn't attract what we desired, huh? Come on, drop this actor God's sake.... Oh Lord! Why can't we learn how to pray, why can't someone teach us the ultimate prayer that is not refusable...."

Upon return from work or waking at some strange hour of the night and at moments when doing research on his dream, he would display this text at his website, read it as if it was the first time, and would look at the commentary of his friends. Each one was a different comedy and a tragedy...

One of his friends wrote, "it must be my fault, I did everything for the million dollars. I visualized such a cheque. I drew it and hung it on my wall. Yesterday a bank notification arrived for due mortgage credit and I lost the house...f'in secret..." And tens of messages similar to this one...

Everyone was being drawn to this new trend with a great dream, doing everything prescribed, but for some reason, the desired outcome was not really happening. He understood why people were being sucked in. Did he not also buy some of these books as a remedy for his search? He would go to church, pray to the Creator but nothing he wanted in his life materialized. Even after repeated prayers, let alone what he wanted, everything he didn't want at all was happening to him. Perhaps there were thousands of people in this situation... And a constant search...

In his most hopeless moments, at moments when his entire self was shaken, he had questioned himself numerous times: "Why isn't the Creator who made everything so perfect seeing me? Why does he not accept my prayers? What is the secret ensuring acceptance of a prayer? If the main reason behind the acceptance of a prayer is the praying person, what is the reason for the denial of most people's prayers? Does the Creator love him and not me?" He asked these questions for years. For some reason, he had first seen that dream one night after beginning to question the Creator rebelliously as a child stuck in these doubts in the days of hopelessness.

Always a search, always a hope since that night... Although not rebelling easily anymore, his entire existence still disappeared among waves of sorrow when his prayers were not answered.

All of a sudden, memories of bad experiences came to his mind. He was saddened... He left the computer. Took the book and stepped into the bedroom. Before long his eyes fell victim to the day's exhaustion and fell asleep with the book still in his hands.

He awakened suddenly, it was past midnight. He looked at the clock on the nightstand, it was 03:27...

A deep inner peace, a joy, but also inexplicable fear...

He had seen the same dream.

The same thing recurred and he was woken up at 03:27.

It was the same thing every single time. This dream was recurring with increasing frequency. It was as if watching the same film over and over again from a DVD. The dream was exactly the same as the one he had seen in his childhood and has been repeating itself for years without the slightest alteration.

The interesting part was that he woke up feeling completely refreshed and alert in the midst of night after seeing this dream. And for some curious reason, the clock always showed 03:27. Not a minute earlier nor later, always 03:27...

He was eleven when he first saw this dream. He had forgotten in time the dream which affected him for a long period. Lost somewhere among the sweet memories of his childhood...

He had seen this dream again when he was seventeen, but this time with a slight difference... He had seen the exact dream at three consecutive nights, woke up suddenly in the midst of the night and found his clock showing 03:27.

He was spending nearly all his time wondering what the dream tried to say.

In his dream he was running fast under the lit street lights through the darkness of the town he grew up in. But this was not a run of escaping, rather running as if to reach at and catch up with something...

Running, running, running, passing through shortcut roads of the town which he knows like the palm of his hand, and speeding down the ramp which he loves most. He enters the narrow road at the end of the downhill ramp and rushes by the old roadside town houses. He knows that he has to see the small old town church at the end of the road. He continues to run....

But when the road ends, he finds himself not in front of the small town church but instead at the edge of a magnificent, large city. Ahead of him lies a great temple...

Looks around, finds himself in a fairly wide square. The temple is enormous. Just watching the magnificence of the building gives him peace. It doesn't look like any other church he has seen until now. A very tall building. With eyes fixed on the temple, he approaches the gate in adoration and awe. As he moves through the temple garden, he sees a domed, beautifully ornamented, embossed pool with the sweet sound of rippling water and surrounding seats. A strange writing around the dome above the pool... Moves slowly toward the interior of the temple. A second gate after the first can be seen. Gates are gigantic. He silently thinks, "The temple must have been built not for humans, but for giants". A mind paralyzing splendor mesmerizes him the moment he enters the large gate. Counts more than ten gates. Door bolts of these gates and metal accessories are pure gold. The dome is unbelievably high and covers the entire temple in a circular line. Impossible not to be awed when confronted with the massiveness of the temple. Sacramental pulpit is very large and pure gold. Bible pedestal is so magnificent and priceless, it's impossible to put in words. There are ten chandeliers from one end to the other. Chandeliers are suspended from the ceiling with silver chains as thick as an arm. Sees a very thick pure gold chain at the center of the dome while gazing at the grandeur of chandeliers. Slowly follows the glitter of the chains downward. At the tip of the chain, seen a globe drowning its surroundings with shimmer. Globe is pure gold and the light from the chandelier candles are reflected off it and scattered everywhere. This is the exact center of the dome and the temple. Light scattered from the golden globe is dazzling. At that moment he sees a human silhouette beneath the globe. Yes, yes, right there, exactly beneath the globe, a person...

Although he can't see his face in the flood of light, wearing a cardigan and a head-cloth shadowing his face, there appears a man...

Saying, "Do you want your prayers accepted? Do you wish to live long on earth? Young and strong... Come to me, I have the secret, find me".

And, as always, the dream ends with this sentence.

Although he usually saw the dream once a year, lately it has been recurring almost every week. Even though frequency of the dream scared him, he also felt certain that something was imminent. He hoped for great wealth... Wealth was his greatest dream since childhood.

Opened his eyes and looked at the clock:03:27...

Mumbled and smiled "What a surprise"...

Once again exactly the same dream... Each moment identical to the previous ones and the time was again 03:27...

Stood, headed directly to the bathroom. Took a warm shower. His mind was fully occupied with the dream....

He was talking to himself, "This time I must find it, must find it today, he wants me to find it. He is calling me". Returned to his room. Powered his computer. He was entering the names of each object in the dream at the Internet search engine and was going through each of the retrieved pages.

Entered the name of the church of his town and surfed tens of pages... He had been going through pages for more than hour now. Tired... Prepared coffee. Took a hot sip. From the window he was gazing at the city lights, questions on his mind, looking while pondering each moment of the dream. Sipped the coffee once more. Dreams and ideas at flight in the darkness of night....

Began thinking of the silhouette he called 'saint' seen in middle of the temple beneath the glare of the golden globe. He couldn't see his face because of the glare. He concluded, "He is a saint". He had a hunch... A voice inside him was telling him this... He is a Saint... He had researched the word saint numerous times online and also in the libraries, and couldn't reach any satisfying result.

This time his mind focused on the saint's silhouette. For one instant it was as if his gaze was frozen and an image struck like a lightning in front of his eyes. The saint was holding a water jug. An earthen water jug... Yes, an earthen water jug in one hand of the saint... Why couldn't he remember this before? How did this sight evade him all this time?

His heart shivered with excitement... Returned fast to his desk. Entered the word "water jug" at the search engine. There were hundreds of pages relating to the "water jug". Began reading the pages from the first website downward. Time flew by. He was still reading the pages. He was entering and exiting internet pages one after the other. One more page and it was as if the title whispered, "what you are looking for is here". He was startled the moment he read the title:

"MAN CARRYING A WATER JUG"

Hundreds of pages were available. But it was as if they were screaming a singular fact...

He began reading the page in haste:

Matthew 26:17-30; Mark 14:12-26

His disciples came to Jesus and asked Him "Where do you want us to make preparations for you to eat the Passover?". Jesus gave an unusual answer. He said unto them: "Go into the city to a certain man and tell him, 'The Teacher says: My appointed time is near. I am going to celebrate the Passover with my disciples at your house'. "Then that man will understand what he must do."

Thus Peter and John went into the city. While walking they saw a MAN CARRYING A WATER JUG (Jesus had described the road going to that house. He said that they would see a man upon entry to the city and they had to follow him and speak of the Passover with the house owner, and that man would be someone carrying a WATER JUG.)

Peter and John walked behind the man until he entered a house. Then they spoke with the house owner about the Passover dinner room. Peter and John said to the man "Our Lord Jesus wants to have Passover feast in your house". Then the owner showed them a large room on the second floor of his house. Disciples cleared the upper room and made it clean as a rose for their Lord's arrival, and waited for Jesus and other disciples.

Later while they were eating, Jesus told them of events which will materialize in times near. Disciples listened to Him with great attention.

Nicholas moved on to another web page:

The Passover Dinner

(Matthew 26:17-35; Mark14:12-31; John 13:21-30, 36-38)

7 - Yeastless Bread day for which Passover sacrifices are required had arrived.

8 - Jesus sent Peter and John ahead with these words: «Go, prepare for the Passover dinner.»

9 - They asked Him, «Where would you want us to make the preparation?»

10-11 Jesus said unto them, «Go and look», «you will meet a MAN CARRYING A WATER JUG. Follow the man until he reaches his house and say thus to the house owner: 'Teacher asks which is the room where he will have Passover dinner with his disciples?'

12 - House owner will show you a large furnished room in the upper floor. Make preparation there.»

13 - Thus they went, and found everything as said to them by Jesus, and made preparation for Passover dinner.

Nicholas was reading all pages with care and excitement. Stood up quickly. He was joyed. Stepped out to the terrace. It was almost morning, as first light of the sun brightened New York he was shouting with happiness:

"I've found you, Saint…"

Months were gone by, as if insane, he was trying to reach information on WATER JUG CARRYING MAN since the day he shouted "I found you saint" at his house terrace. To this end, he had travelled to England, Germany, France and Vatican, and spent days sifting through valuable hand-written books in the most famous libraries of the world. Even though the failure to reach a satisfactory result had discouraged him, he still carried on with research with anew excitement nearly every morning. Because now he was seeing the dream every night and every night he was waking up at 03:27.

Why would Jesus describe the house of Passover dinner in such a strange way...

Yes, yes, obviously Jesus put the man at the forefront for his disciples instead of describing the house, he was as if pointing at the man. Why didn't Jesus describe the house in a normal way? Why didn't he describe it in a familiar way saying, "walk along the street after entering the city, turn right at the narrow road, you will see a high building with three floors, or as, the one next to the last house on the street", and instead said "you will see a MAN CARRYING A WATER JUG upon entry to the city, follow him".

Why did Jesus say "follow the MAN CARRYING A WATER JUG"? Obviously Jesus knew things and did not say it openly. As if he hid it from some, but still ciphered the information for identification. Did he hide it because he knew what was going to happen after that evening's Passover dinner? He knew there was a traitor amongst them. He did speak of this treachery during the evening. Did he hide it because he knew that traitor would also reveal the MAN CARRYING A WATER JUG"? As if he hid it from evil eyes and ciphered it to be found later. Nicholas sometimes neared insanity amidst such thoughts and unanswered questions. For hours and even days he was struggling with these thoughts.

Nicholas decided to go on the weekend to the pretty town of his birth and teenage years. Relieving some yearning with his parents could be very good for him. Also, it might be helpful to see the priest in the town and tell him what has been happening. When at a much younger age, he had already spoken to the priest of this dream. He took off hoping that priest might say a few helpful things.

A run on a beautiful spring morning in this small childhood town invigorated Nicholas. He was examining his surroundings along the road where he ran in his dreams. Hope of a sign was always drawing him to this route. Each time he was finding himself in front of the pretty church, talking a little with the priest and returning home. It had been a week since his arrival. It was bothering to have found nothing.

Since the day of his arrival, he rose up in early morning and ran along the same road in his dreams. In reality now he was exercising. The excess body weight was a problem for him. He mumbled to himself, "only ten years ago I was able to run this road and back several times. Now I can only run half of it and walk the other half". He was short of breath as he said it.

He was in front of the church located at the end of the road. Exhausted, he sat at the edge of the fountain basin in the luscious green garden of the church. Having seen Nicholas, the priest came by smiling. Two warm friends hugged with sincerity. He began talking about the "man carrying a water jug". Again he couldn't understand how time flew by. It was almost evening. After bidding farewell to the priest, he began walking home on the same road, absorbed in his thoughts, the road on which he ran in his dream. He was sad.... He still couldn't find anything. What is more, the priest couldn't contribute even a small thing to the solution. He only said, "Wait, be patient, this is a great tiding, I think in time the secret will be revealed". "I have been waiting for years, how much longer?" he answered desperately,

Upon returning home, he found his parents talking in the garden. Sat beside them smiling. While talking about the day his mother said, "Son, you left your phone behind, I was worried. It rang numerous times, someone called you insistently, maybe you should go check it". He said "probably my friends, I don't think it is anything important, mother".

Left them and went inside. Looked at his phone. There were forty missed calls. The caller was his friend Michael from work. Michael was his best friend. He knew everything about his life, even the details of his recurring dream. He was aware of his related trips and ongoing research. He had accompanied him several times to England and Vatican. While Nicholas was struggling amongst hand-written books in the libraries, Michael was having fun as a tourist.

"Something important must have happened, why else would he call me so many times", he thought. Immediately called Michael. Before he could utter a single word:

"Where the hell are you, man?" asked Michael.

With a concerned voice, Nicholas said:

"Did something happen to you?"

"Today somebody came by and asked about you. Look pal, this man might be in the know."

"Who came, what does he know, speak straight".

"Someone in a suit. A library director. Asked about you. I told him you were on a leave. He said you were researching at all the wrong places. What you are looking for is apparently in Jerusalem".

"What kind of a man was he? Didn't you get his name? Which library's director?"

In shock Nicholas lined up the questions.

Michael said, "I am sorry buddy, when the man finished his words, I asked him who he was and how he knew of you. The man smiled and said, "We know him well but he is searching at the wrong place. What he is looking for is in Jerusalem". Then he quickly left the office. I went after him, but believe me pal, when I reached the corridor, he was nowhere to be seen. I got on the elevator, went outside of the building, but it was as if he disappeared in an instant."

Not knowing what to say, Nicholas remained silent on the phone for a while in surprise. Silence was broken by Michael's voice on the other end of the line.

"Nicholas, what are you planning to do? Who is this man? Look buddy, until now I thought of your research as an adventure caused by fixation at a dream. OK, I have been supportive of you, but now, I don't know, this business turned weird. This goes beyond the mysteries mentioned in novels and movies. "

Michael went quiet as if to wait for Nicholas to say a thing or two. Nicholas was awed.

Again he asked, "Buddy, what kind of a man was he? Where did he know of me? How did he know I was researching?"

Wanting to suggest a solution, Michael:

"A library director. An old man. A very polite, likeable person. You've made research in lots of libraries. While asking for books, did you ever mention your research or your dream to any library director?"

Nicholas uttered:

"I just said I was researching books about the man carrying a water jug who is mentioned in the Bible".

Michael, as if he had solved the problem, retorted:

"Well, now you see. Probably it was a library director who knew this. Later he heard something about the subject. I think he just came to inform you".

Nicholas:

"OK, let's assume that it is true. But how did he learn where I was working? I never mentioned at any library where I worked or lived".

The silence ensued showed that neither Nicholas nor Michael had any response to this question.

Nicholas said "Buddy, let me think a little and call you back" and shut the phone.

His heart was beating with trepidation since the moment he landed at the airport. It was the first time he had arrived in a country unknown and unseen before for the resolution of a mystery… As the cab from the airport speeded to the city center, his thoughts, dreams, feelings and what is more, his worries of being in a country he did not know were all mixed up.

The cab jerked with a sudden stop as if to say they had arrived. A smiling hotel attendant took his luggage from the cab. After a short formality at the reception, he proceeded to the elevator together with the attendant carrying his luggage.

After departure of the attendant from the room, he stepped toward the window. He was on the soil where Jesus lived, not only that, he was where the mysterious MAN CARRYING A WATER JUG had lived. As he was gazing the unique scenery of Jerusalem, his mind was under the captivity of strange intoxicating feelings.

This was one of the quarters of Eastern Jerusalem. He had especially chosen this hotel. If there was a sign, then this was the correct place to be. Because after the Passover dinner, this was the place where Jesus came with his disciples... The last dinner was had in one of those houses he could see from the window and after the last dinner, Jesus came where he now was with his disciples. On Mount Olive, in his hotel room, he was looking at Jerusalem.

He came to Jerusalem with an impulsive decision. He couldn't sleep all night after his phone conversation with Michael. Called Michael numerous times during the night, asked questions about the library director and had him repeat what had happened. He thought until dawn. He had no time to lose. "Forget who he is, he is talking about something special like your dream. I have to use this opportunity..." and after bidding farewell to his parents early in the morning he returned to New York. Without any delays and having met Michael briefly, he headed to the airport on the same day for a flight to Jerusalem.

Even though he didn't know exactly what he had to do or where to begin researching, he was aware that there were many places to investigate in Jerusalem. The Holy Grave Church located where Jesus was crucified after he was forced to march by the Romans along the Via Dolores with a wooden cross on his back, The Church of Punishment where Roman soldiers placed a thorned crown on the head of Prophet Jesus, St. Anna Church built in place of the house of Virgin Mary's parents, Russian and Greek Orthodox church, holy place of Ethiopian Catholics, The Holy Sepulchre Church and many other holy places....

In short, places to be investigated in Jerusalem were numerous and just as important. But for Nicholas the most important one was the house where Jesus had the Passover Dinner, the last dinner he ate. The most important lead, if there was any, about the "Man Carrying a Water Jug" should be at that house. In order to find a trace, he must find the exact location of that house. He was convinced that whatever building was there now, there had to be a lead.

The trip from New York, the questions occupying his mind, the identity of the library director which twisted his brain had extremely exhausted him. He laid down for a rest on the large bed of his hotel room, his eyes couldn't resist exhaustion anymore and closed.

He suddenly rose up, the clock was showing 03:27. He was accustomed to seeing the same dream and waking up at this hour. He stepped out to his room balcony. Facing him was a silent city filled with mysteries yet to be revealed to him. He was at an important point. The Mount Olive....

The first lights of the sun lit Jerusalem, but Nicholas was already walking the city like a tourist.

Hassidics walking fast as if trying to avoid other people, white robed Arabs, women with white headscarves, men and women Israeli soldiers with modern weapons, Christians who came for pilgrimage from all corners of the world and Jews visiting the crying wall...

Nicholas was amazed. This was a different country.

He had begun touring the city at the Mount Olive where his hotel was. It was nearly impossible for him to describe his feelings to another person. Mount Olive was the place where the Messiah would arrive and last judgment would be done.

Romans caught Jesus on the slopes of Mount Olive where he held his final sermon. Nicholas was now in front of the All Nations Church built on the stone where Jesus gave his last sermon. At the column crowns of the church were olive tree figurines. Because of the olive trees in its garden, this place was named Gethsemane.

After a brief visit of the church and a prayer, Nicholas went ahead touring the city with curiosity.

Eight gates surrounded the Old City. The Golden Gate facing the Mount Olive was closed with stone masonry. In ancient texts Nicholas had read that the Messiah would enter the city from this gate. He passed through the Japha Gate, second in significance, arrived at the location known as Western Wall by the Jews, and Wailing Wall by the Christians. The remaining wall of the second temple torn down for the final time in 70 AD was filled with crying Jews at every hour of day and night. Hassidics, in other words, extreme fundamentalist Jews, with their long curled hairs, black hats, white shirts and black suits were moving fast toward the wall as if they had entered the pull of a magnet. Children among them with their clothing and curls were like copies of their fathers.

Women and men wanting to touch and kiss the western wall were crying separately at the yard divided by a portable screen.

Jews or others were squeezing into whatever holes they could find pieces of paper bearing their wishes. Right away Nicholas wrote down on piece of paper his wish for wealth and softly squeezed it into a small hole. He learned that the chief rabbi of Jerusalem collected these papers from the wall holes and buried them in the Mount Olive. It was believed that God read these messages.

It was noon and the tour of city had tired Nicholas and made him hungry. He entered the first local restaurant he could find and had his fill. After the restaurant he entered Via Dolorosa where Jesus had walked carrying his cross. He started walking along a little perturbed thinking, "If I recollect, the longest and bloodiest scene in Mel Gibson's film 'The Passion of the Christ' was about the walk on this road". The places where Jesus had fallen from time to time while walking were called stations where churches were built. Along the way, there are 14 stations, five of which are at the Holy Grave Church. Each friday, Franciscan priests walk the same route trying to experience the agony of Jesus.

Alongside of this holy road, everything is sold on tables erected. Belly dancer attire, seven-armed candle holders (menorah), offering candles, pilgrimage knick knacks and pictures of Jesus carrying the cross among many other things…

Mumbled to himself, "Jesus's agony has been transformed into trade". Still he walked the road trying to feel Christ's trials and tribulations. He couldn't refrain from thinking, "I wonder if Jesus was to see this road now, what would he do?". When he reached the top, he was at Jerusalem's poorest but most original church, the Ethiopian Catholic Church. Several Ethiopian priests were engaged in a deep conversation. At the yard of the Holy Grave Church next door candidate priests were gathered in a corner listening to their teacher. Hyms of the women pilgrims from Russia were mixing with the voices of the American group at the opposite corner repeating the prayer of a minister.

The entrance of church and the vicinity of the stone which was presumed to be the place where Jesus had been washed after being lowered from the cross were thick with crowd. Those kissing the stone, those crying, and those who were trying to receive favors from Jesus by rubbing to stone the water, beads and holy books were in a state of trance.

Nicholas gently entered the line up for the Holy Grave. Passed through a dark gallery and entered the small space a few steps below. Impossible to see inside the glassed section, lit a candle, began praying. Grave was covered with a massive stone placed there in 19th Century.

He exited from behind the Holy Grave through a section belonging to the Assyrian Church. All day long he had conversations with the religious men of churches. What his real curiosity was the location of the house where Jesus had his Passover dinner which became the subject of Da Vinci's painting. What was now in place of that house?

The clergy men Nicholas spoke with guided him to one direction only. The target now was the Dormition Church built in place of Levi's house on Mount Zion where Jesus is presumed to have had his last dinner.

Nicholas had always assumed that there would be a church there instead of a house. "A place as important as that couldn't have been converted into something else," he thought. He moved quickly in anticipation of seeing the church at once. The possibility excited him. He walked as if on the run while thinking, "there, an evidence, a sign or a lead must exist about the man carrying a water jug".

A little later the Dormition Church was visible on the hill. "Resembles a castle," he thought. As he neared the building, he felt an odd shiver. Church really put up a sight like a castle on Mount Zion with its conical dome and towers.

Nicholas entered tensely. Those being photographed, crying, groups singing hymns were creating a bustle. He was unable to visualize the twelve disciples, the long dining table, Judas who would sequel on Jesus and sitting with his back to the table, in short, Leonardo da Vinci's painting of the last dinner and Tiziano's denunciation scene. Because in the church there were no identifiable symbols relating to such an important slice of time ever having been lived… Hidden as it were… This church had been constructed later upon the ruins of a previous one.

On his first day in Dormition, he spent hours inching every part of the church. His spirit had taken flight. He was immersed in strange feelings. He kept repeating, "Here it is... Man carrying a water jug came here. Jesus had his last dinner here. It's all here".

As he paced, Nicholas was perturbed at every step because of the importance of the place. His guts recoiled, an inexplicable wave of wonder covered his soul. Location of Jesus' last dinner, the place where the man with a jug had arrived and King David's grave just around the corner… Nicholas was taken with the storm of indefinable emotions.

Since his first arrival in Jerusalem, early everyday Nicholas left his hotel at Mount Olive, observantly walked over to the location of the last dinner on Mount Zion and stayed all day long at this place. Sometimes he just watched the Dormition Church for hours, sank in thoughts and questions, and sometimes he looked for a sign, an evidence however small inside the building.

"Here where this church is located something very important took place. Last dinner was very important. Jesus came here knowing that there was a traitor among them. Not only that, he sent disciples ahead for the Passover dinner preparation. The house was shown to the disciples by the man carrying a water jug just as Jesus had said. Very important things happened here. Things of significance we do not know, discussions took place here".

While he walked around all day long, he was agonizing among the thoughts and questions with no answers. Sometimes there were moments when Nicholas just wanted to scream, "Who are you, Man Carrying a Water Jug, who are you?"

It was the twenty-seventh day of his arrival in Jerusalem. For twenty-seven days he had been examining every inch of the area where the last dinner was held. He was hoping to find an old scribble, a sign or a cipher. Man carrying the water jug had said to him 'find me', and then perhaps he must have left something written at that time. He also knew that this was a false hope. This church had been constructed over a previous one. For this reason, Nicholas was searching for a sign in the immediate area. The sun was overhead at noon. He sat in a corner of the church garden, exhausted from searching the interior, exterior and surroundings of the church, and impatient. He caught himself uttering aloud perhaps due to nervousness, tiredness or some other thing. Several tourists passed him by smiling. He didn't care. His gaze turned again to the church. Seated, he was distanced while gazing at the rooster figurine atop the bell tower. He was jerked with a gloomy voice which said, "He, too, awaits you". Right away he turned toward the voice behind him. An aged priest in dark attire was standing.

"Excuse me, did you say something?"

Smiling, the priest said, "Yes, son, I spoke to you".

In that moment's confusion and not knowing exactly what to say, Nicholas apologetically and courteously said, "I couldn't understand what you meant". The priest with an extremely gentle tone said, "He awaits you".

Failing to grasp it, Nicholas responded in surprise, "I am sorry, but I think you are mixing me with someone else. I came from New York. There is no one here who would wait for me".

Man touched him over the shoulder smiling, took a step or two, stopped and turned to look at Nicholas.

"Did you not a moment ago say 'who are you'?".

A little embarrassed, Nicholas fixed his eyes away from the priest and thought "Hell, I must have been thinking aloud again, pull yourself together Nicholas, you're making a fool of yourself ".

He said to the priest, "I was just mumbling away".

Man in the black robe took a few steps, turned again and said, "If you are wondering about him, be here tonight at 3:27". Turned around, immediately joined a tourist group and walked fast toward the church.

At that moment Nicholas froze up. Who was this man? What did this all mean now? It was as if 03:27 was one of the most private secrets of his life. The words thoroughly mixed him up. He pulled himself together fast and ran after the man toward the church. He looked around for a long time in a state of daze. The man was not there. In a few seconds, the man vanished into thin air!

Hours knew not how to elapse. Nicholas anxiously waited for midnight in trepidation. "Who was that man? Would it be correct to go to the Dormition Church at a strange hour? What if something nasty happens?"

Nicholas was agonizing in his thoughts at his hotel room. His mind spewed questions for which he had no answers. "Either I must leave at once for New York or follow this deal to the end wherever it leads" he pondered, and his conclusion was to pursue it. He stepped out of the hotel decidedly, and walked the distance to the church with heavy feet. It was exactly 03:20 when he arrived at the entrance gate of the church. He was just standing in front of it at this strange hour of the night. Curiosity and fear in entanglement was frying up his entire self. His eyes were on his wrist watch and the church gate. A short while later, the gate opened noisily in the midst of the night darkness. A man's silhouette appeared at the gate. Nicholas' heart was beating furiously. "Is that him? Could he be the Man Carrying a Water Jug?"

Nicholas answered his own question at once in his mind: "Stop it Nicholas, be sensible, that man lived at the time of Jesus. Sure as hell he is dead. Centuries ago..."

Man at the church gate was walking slowly toward Nicholas. Nicholas took a look at the time, it was 03:27. When they met, he instantly recognized the man. He was the same man who had just today said, "He, too, awaits you" and disappeared.

Man in the same robe said welcome. Nicholas was in fear and curiosity. Not knowing what to do, he just laid the questions one after another: "Who are you? You said 'he too awaits you'. Who awaits me?"

With a smile barely noticeable in the darkness, the old man said, "The one you are looking for". Nicholas was looking with empty eyes at the old man and the words, "I am not looking for anyone. I am only searching information about the Man Carrying a Water Jug mentioned in the Bible" poured out of him.

Old man's hand reached forward holding a ribboned roll, Nicholas asked what it was while taking it hesitantly.

The old man responded saying, "The time has arrived for certain things. My duty ends here. You are holding a map. Dig where the map shows. What you are going to find will shed light into your search". As he was speaking, he suddenly held his chest and fell on his knees with a slight moaning and rattling sound in his throat. Terrified, Nicholas grabbed the man.

"What happened, is there something wrong? Speak, please, are you OK?"

Just he was attempting to scream for help, the old man held Nicholas by the right shoulder saying:

"Be calm. My job is over. I am at peace. I have done what I was required to do. I have waited your arrival for years to hand over to you this charge of trust. Now I can pass on. Beware Nicholas, never give up searching for him. He awaits you. It is very difficult to journey with him", and then he collapsed.

In terror and confusion, Nicholas quickly clasped the old man not knowing what to do. He was intensely shaking the man while shouting, "Are you OK? Just speak, will you?"

Shuddering, touched the old man in the neck where his main arteries are. When he realized the man was dead, he stayed frozen for a while which seemed like eternity. Then he suddenly jumped up and began running like mad. As he ran, the only thing he can think was, "what if they think I killed him?"

When he arrived at the hotel, his heart was beating out of his chest. He was breathing heavily. He began gathering his things the moment he entered his room. He was scared to death. Kept saying, "What the hell am I doing here?" He wasn't able to stop his hands from trembling. His legs were also shaking. Just as he finished stuffing his luggage, he noticed the ribboned roll thrown on the bed. He had forgotten the map while in fear of a man dying in his hands. For a moment or two he hesitated about unrolling the map. He knew himself too well... If he opened the map, then he would be sure to pursue it. Hesitated tensely a while longer. Then untied the ribbon, gently and slowly spread the rolled map flat on the bed. The paper was obviously very old. Drawings on it and the arrow signs were pointing at something buried. Perplexed, a little collected and calm, his eyes lit up with fear and hope at the same time...

Digging hard ground in the midst of night with a small adze was very difficult. But bringing a bigger pickaxe would have drawn attention and got him in trouble, so he had purchased the small adze during the day, and placed it in a small bag hoping it would go unnoticed. He had gotten the bag from a store he had been shopping and carried the adze in it. He was fairly tired. Wiped his forehead and stood up. On the Mount Olive, near a yard with hundreds of graves just beneath it, he was digging the earth like a treasure hunter in the middle of the night. Full moon was transforming nearly everything into a sight in twilight. The fear of being caught shivered his heart.

His mind was still on what took place the night before. He was thinking of the words of the old man who just died in the garden of the Dormition Church, and was trying to comprehend them. The man said that his duty was over, having done what was required he would die in peace, and had been waiting for years to deliver his charge to Nicholas.

Nicholas was trapped by these words. While digging the ground in fear he kept repeating: "Why would anyone wait for me? I am nobody. He waited years for me? My God, I am not someone who should be waited for".

He was tired. He was digging the spot for more than an hour now. He had dug a large pit at the base of the tree. Stopped briefly. Looked around carefully and listened. Once again the sights of the previous night hit him. The old man had said, "Beware Nicholas, never give up searching for him, He awaits you, it is very difficult to journey with Him."

The person the old man called "He"; could he be the Man Carrying a Water Jug? Were they talking about the same person? No, that wouldn't be possible. That person lived at the time of Jesus. He couldn't possibly still be alive. He sure as hell must have died long ago. These thoughts were almost drowning Nicholas.

"Fine. That priest at the church. I don't even know his name. Who the hell was he talking about before he died? Who is waiting for me? Journeying with him is very difficult. What journey? To where?".

Then he noticed he was thinking aloud once again. He continued digging while wondering: "Terrific, really great, here I am digging the ground near a grave yard, near a holy church, on Mount Olive, and I am carrying on a conversation with myself, terrific..." The wooden handle of the adze was seriously paining the palm of his gloveless right hand. There was a chance, wouldn't he know it, sure enough it would soon blister and he won't be able to dig any more. The idea of having to leave the place with a sore hand and nothing to show for it just didn't appeal to his ambitious nature.

All of a sudden, when the adze hit a hard object most unexpectedly, he was shocked to his bones. His heart was beating furiously...

His initial thought was that it might be a rock and he dug around it a little more. His left hand on the pit edge, body bending downward when he cleared the loose soil around it with his hurting arm and hand while on his knees, he noticed the geometric shape of a man-made object. He was feeling the discomfort of the rough, sharp gravel, clay soil under his finger nails. Hand hurting more, he struggled a short while with the object, forced it backward and sideways to loosen it further from its location where only God knows how long it had remained buried.

Pulled it out quickly. It was a small chest covered in dirt. Its exterior felt hard and strong. He moved quickly, rubbed the excess soil off, in near darkness felt a small and thoroughly rusted padlock on the chest. He placed the chest on firm flat ground near the pit, still on his knees and with gentle moon light striking the chest, he broke the padlock with several careful but strong blows, fearing the noise it might make.

He was awed, maybe he was he about to be rich… What lay in this decorated chest? Forced it open and in it he felt something wrapped in cloth. He unwrapped the dirty yellowish cloth with care. What he had in his hand was a book. A masterfully decorated book in perfect shape like those of old empires… Since its unwrapping, the book was glittering under weak moonlight. The reason for the shimmer on book was golden gilded ornamentation. On the cover of the book were beautiful writings in an ancient language calligraphed masterfully. He was able to read the larger writing. He was happy to be able to do so. While struggling with old handwritten manuscripts for years in libraries, he had noticed his deficiency and attended ancient language and writings courses. He was now able to read the name of the book written with golden gilt on the cover of the book: THE BOOK OF SECRETS.

His heart was beating like mad. He placed the book in the shopping bag he had brought along. Carefully but quickly cleared the soil and dirt of the bag, his hands, knees of his pants, elbow of his right-arm shirt sleeve. Took a deep breath, carefully looked around once more, and trying to control his excitement, he quickly headed toward the hotel. He treated the handsome but now heavier bag hanging from his left hand like he would any other during a casual shopping day. While he walked past the shop windows, he briefly stopped several times not to look at items on sale but instead to check his reflection on the glass and to settle his emotions down. Finally calm, he entered the hotel. Smiled gently at the receptionist, took his room card and walked to the elevator. He felt as if the elevator was not moving but he knew that in moments this madness will be over. He walked fast to his room in the carpeted and nicely lit floor corridor. Entered the room and locked the door. Turned on all the lights, closed the curtains. Pulled out the book. Now the magnificence of the book was all the more visible. Decorations of the cover were incredible. The book glittered in the room light. His anxiety for seeing the first page turned into an unbelievable disappointment when he gently flipped the cover open. He flipped a few more pages carefully but rather impatiently. He was absolutely shocked. He couldn't understand. He mumbled, "How could this be? What does this mean now?"

Individually all the pages were fairly thick. But this was not its only difference from other regular books.... All its pages had been completely darkened black. Even more surprising thing was that pages didn't seem to contain a single line of writing. This was ridiculous. How could a book like this be of black pages? How could it be empty?

Nicholas was pacing back and forth meaninglessly in the room not knowing what to do next. At one moment while glimpsing with a cool head at the mirror on the wall, he nervously giggled, "What the hell does this mean now? A beautiful book with empty, black pages... Why not leave them blank and white..."

He was upset and tired from digging like a fool in the midst of the night in a strange and dangerous land. "I better take a shower," he thought.

Warm shower water was like a gift from heavens, but he kept thinking about the meaning of the dark and empty pages of the book. A little while later, he stepped out of shower. Not finding what he was expecting must have discouraged his will to struggle and diminished his excitement. He didn't even bother to dry his hair. Wet and with water droplets hitting the floor, he walked to his bed. He just didn't care about anything anymore. He looked at the shimmering book on the table. Took a few wet steps on the carpeted floor and touched the book with his finger tip and flipped the cover without any hope. Angrily he mumbled, "What a terrific cover for empty pages". He leaned forward and a small drop of water fell on the page while he was looking at the blackened page. Suddenly something miraculous happened. He saw a momentary gentle light beam before several brightly colored words began appearing on the page:

"IN THE BEGINNING GOD CREATED THE HEAVEN AND EARTH.

EARTH WAS VOID, FORMLESS, COVERED WITH ENDLESS DARKNESS.

GOD'S SPIRIT MOVED ON WATERS…"

In confusion, Nicholas dropped the book. Reached down and took the book back with strange emotions.

How could this be? A droplet or two and there you are... Suddenly words on the page?

He read it once more, then again.... His confusion increased. He already knew these words by heart. But he couldn't understand how these words appeared all at once.

He grabbed the water glass on the table, hasted to the bathroom sink, filled the glass with water and returned. Wetted his finger tips in the glass and flipped to the next page. Gently sprinkled droplets.

Same light beam appeared on that page, too. A decorative gentle writing appeared slowly: WATER...

"It needs more," he thought. Sprinkled more droplets. Nothing happened. No light beam. Writing unchanged... Compared to the first page, this was a weaker appearing writing as if on the back plan of the page. It was as if a writing silhouette beneath others: WATER...

Wetted his finger tips again, flipped to the next page, and carefully sprinkled. The light beam reappeared and the writings followed it soon enough. Same thing happened on this page as well. The same writing on the background covered the entire page: WATER...

He did the same thing over and over at every page. He wetted his finger tips and sprinkled water droplets to all of the three hundred and twenty seven pages. The result was always the same. First a sweet beam of light; then the large writing: WATER.

Tired and on the last page, he sprinkled a few droplets thinking, "The same thing will also happen here". The beam of light... While he was waiting for the word "Water" to appear, a point on the page was formed and it slid fast down the length of the page and created a straight line. Nicholas was trembling. The point continued its rapid movement on the page. His brain, emotions, thoughts and soul were paralyzed, even the time froze. His whole body numb, the book in his hand, Nicholas was looking in awe to the figure forming on the page. A brief moment later he began repeating, "Oh my God, oh my God". He was utterly shocked and confused.

The point's fast ceremonial movement on the page continued with the sweet beam of light in front of his eyes, and the moment point ceased motion, there appeared a picture on the page. Once again he dropped the book in excitement. Bent quickly, grabbed the book and reopened the last page. The temple he had seen in his dreams repeatedly since childhood was there, right on the last page, with all details.

A word had appeared under the formed picture: Hagia Sophia.

At the bottom of the page he saw a much smaller writing. He leaned forward and carefully looked at it. He could read what appeared to be a signature: Da Vinci.

His body paralyzed and his soul frozen, he was stuck there just looking at the book in a great, indescribable amazement. It was as if the time too had stopped. He just couldn't think any more...

Well now, was this book also written by Da Vinci? A book which would reveal itself with droplets of water could only be written by him, who else? If this is really a Da Vinci book he thought, "sure as hell I am rich now". "I must return to New York right away" and straightened up in joy. But for some reason he stopped gathering his things within a few moments. The repeating dreams which had been more frequent in recent years, all of it, it was everything for this book only? "Why not?" he thought, "When it is understood that the book is Da Vinci's, God knows how many millions of bucks it will be worth".

"But the picture on the last page… The temple I've been seeing in my dreams."

Could it be that the man carrying a water jug in his dreams for years on end wanted him to find and sell the book? "He is a saint; it can never be for such a simple purpose" and slowly lay on the bed. After all the research he had done over time, he felt a lot of respect to the Man Carrying a Water Jug. "He is a wonderful person, for sure he must have spoken with Jesus. Jesus described the house of the Passover dinner to his disciples through him. No, I still don't know what he wants". He stood up quickly and began circling the room talking to himself in wonder. At one moment he stopped. He said, "what was he saying to me in my dream?"

"Do you wish the acceptance of your prayers? Do you want to live long? Strong and young... Come to me, I have the secret, come find me."

Thoughts in his mind were battling. One side was saying, "Go back to New York, this is Da Vinci's book. Sell it. Be wealthy". The other side was saying, "Man Carrying a Water Jug asked if you wanted your prayers honored. 'I have the secret, find me' he said. He wouldn't come into your dreams for such a stupid thing, you must still find him". That old man who died in your arms in the middle of the night at church garden said, "I was waiting for you. I delivered my charge. Now I can die in peace". "One more thing… The Man Carrying a Water Jug couldn't possibly be alive now, but there must be something, something much more important".

He paced for few hours here and there in his room not knowing what he could do. Looked at the time, it was almost dawn. Opened the curtains. The very first lights of the day were brightening Jerusalem. He stepped out to the small balcony facing the city. He was observing the city with complicated and mixed feelings. On one half of his brain, The Man Carrying a Water Jug; on the other Da Vinci. While looking at the city from the balcony, he jumped on his feet, quickly entered the room, and powered his computer. He was acting with the certainty of having discovered something. On his search engine page he wrote: Hagia Sophia.

Ascended stairs to the airplane with an indescribable feeling. He was headed to an unknown. Departing from Jerusalem. In him there was a weird sorrow equaling the feelings he had at his initial arrival. Took his seat in the plane. All he lived passed through his mind like a film strip. What he had gone through lately was unbelievable. His mind was still preoccupied with what the priest had said before his death and the incredible night at the Dormition Church. After the treasure-hunter like dig on the Mount Olive with the map given by the priest, he was now on an aircraft the same morning. He tightly held the invaluable Book of Secrets he had dug out at the Mount Olive on his lap as if it was a gift package. The drawing which appeared on the last page of the book was the picture of the temple he had dreamt about for many years. *Hagia Sophia* was written below the picture. In his hotel room at dawn, he had searched Hagia Sophia on the internet and he was paralyzed in the sight of images that appeared on his computer screen. He was unable to think anything and just stared at the screen in a daze. Only after a while, was he able to say, "The temple in my dream really exists as is". He was excitedly mesmerized with hundreds of

Hagia Sophia images which kept coming up on his screen. Now he was on the airplane to Istanbul, the home of Hagia Sophia. After all that happened to him in the recent years, he came to conceive unexpected ideas, embark on unexpected journeys with a mad courage and jump on adventures.

Upon learning that Hagia Sophia was located in Istanbul, he grabbed the phone to the hotel reception, asked them to arrange a plane ticket to Istanbul, and to ready the check-out bill. Then he downloaded as much Hagia Sophia information as possible to his laptop.

As he was immersed in mysterious information, his phone ring brought Nicholas to his senses. The receptionist was on the line, "Sir, there is a flight to Istanbul in two hours departing at 11 AM, do you wish me to arrange the ticket?" Nicholas thanked politely and asked for the purchase of a ticket. He took a cab to the airport. He was suddenly shaken with the driver's voice, "We are here, sir". When he looked over, he saw that they were at the terminal entrance gate. He had been so absorbed with the Hagia Sophia information on his laptop that he hadn't even taken a slight look at Jerusalem he was leaving behind. He felt a little guilty.

After a flight of over two hours, he landed at the Istanbul Ataturk Airport. He quickly headed to a cab. The driver loaded his luggage into the trunk of the cab. Sympathetic driver was speaking fairly fluent English. Identifying himself as 'Selim', the driver began telling Nicholas about Istanbul as they slowly rolled out of the airport.

As Selim was saying, "If you like, I can show you around in Istanbul. Well, not a day, not even a life time is enough to see it all anyway"… "Excuse me, can you take me to a hotel which has the full view of the Hagia Sophia and located in the vicinity?" Nicholas interrupted.

"OK, we will take the shore highway; from there we will reach the Sultan Ahmed area. There I know a pretty boutique hotel which sees the Hagia Sophia in full. I recommend it" said Selim. Upon approval of Nicholas by saying "That'll be very good", Selim headed for the route. Nicholas was watching the adjacent sea flowing. A wave of excitement was running deep through him.

He was about to see the temple in his dreams. This was a strange, different city. The city appeared divided by the sea flowing next to him as the cab followed the shoreline. Opposing shore was the continent of Asia as they were in the continent of Europe. A channel of flowing water in-between... Yes, exactly, a sea was flowing between the two sides of the city. Not a river... A channel connecting the Black Sea to the north, to the Marmara then Aegean to the south... A neck of water separating both continents. The "Bosphorous" in mythology...

When the cab left the shoreline road and turned uphill, his excitement climaxed. The cab climbed uphill among the old Istanbul buildings. It was moving slowly in traffic on the narrow streets. Then quickly turned on to a narrow alley between two shops selling touristic gifts. Moved a little further and stopped. While the cab driver Selim looked back and said, "This is the hotel I mentioned earlier. You can take a peek at the rooms and if you don't like it, we can search another hotel. But this is the hotel with the best view of the Hagia Sophia", for Nicholas looking where Selim pointed, the notion of time had evaporated and Selim's words were merely a buzz. The temple he had seen in his dreams for years was now just ahead of him...

Nicholas, under the spell of Hagia Sophia, woke up with the gentle voice of the hotel doorman: "Welcome, sir". With his gaze locked on the temple, he followed the doorman.

This was small, but a cute hotel. Nicholas asked for a room with a view of Hagia Sophia. On his way to the room, he was as if in a different planet. Upon entry to the room, Nicholas quickly headed to the window. When he opened the curtains, he was confronted with a magnificent scene beyond his expectations. Although Hagia Sophia was not very far, it stood as if right in front of him. He stepped out to the small balcony of his room. It was as if the view in front of him called Nicholas into another world.

Seated at the balcony table, he was looking at Hagia Sophia for an extended period. He was very tired. He had gone through incredible days. Only the night before, he had dug at the Mount Olive and found a book at the base of a tree. After a sudden decision following a sleepless night, he was now here. Even though he was exhausted, Hagia Sophia appeared to be calling him.

Nicholas entered his room. He placed the "Book of Secrets" into the ciphered case in his room and locked it. Without touching his luggage, he left the hotel for Hagia Sophia located a very short distance away.

After a short walk, he was on a spacious square in front of the temple. It was crowded. It was possible to see people from all corners of the world. Tourist groups had formed long waiting lines for entry to Hagia Sophia. Not very pleased, Nicholas also joined a line. Finally it was his turn. Excitedly he took his visitation card and entered the garden of Hagia Sophia.

Now he was about to enter the temple he'd repeatedly dreamt about. There were several doors after the main gate. Just as in his dream, he counted nine doors. Nine doors opening to the interior. The largest was said to be left over from Noah's Ark. Nicholas headed to this main gate. It was enormous and very thick. Touching it was pleasant. He had seen it in his dream. He recalled thinking about it in his dream as "must be for giants". He passed through in mixed strange feelings. It was impossible to describe the ambiance of the interior. This was an incredible place. Temple had a very large dome. The angelic figurines at the base perimeter of the dome immediately attracted his attention. The ornamentation of the sphinxes was magnificent. He walked toward the center of the dome. It was as if something was continuously turning his head upward. He stepped forward slowly looking at the round dome. Now he was exactly at the point where in his dream he had seen the "man carrying a water jug". At the exact center of the temple, beneath the dome. Precisely at this point in his dream, there was a large golden globe suspended with a gold chain from the dome above. Naturally, Nicholas was not expecting to find the golden globe or the chains. During the European Crusaders' invasion, the temple was ransacked, which he learnt about after a brief internet research. How odd was it that the Crusaders in search of the "Holy Grail" had centuries ago ransacked this renowned temple of the time.

Every point in the temple had a very fine mason workmanship. The structure was completely adorned with ornamentation and art. Very tall columns supported the temple. The small windows at the ceiling permitted in pleasant rays of the sun and added a different ambiance to the spell-bound interior. Looking at the dome above was mesmerizing for Nicholas. He was filled with incredible feelings. The joy of finding the real-world temple he dreamt about repeatedly over the years and now to be walking in it was not a pleasure put into words so easily.

The interior of Hagia Sophia was packed. Hundreds of people from all around the world filled the place to its capacity. Japanese, Germans, British, Russians and many more....

Spell-bound, Nicholas began pacing the interior of the temple. Toward the entrance, in the section to the left of the structure, he saw people who had formed a long queue in front of a temple column. He approached them in curiosity. There was a hole at the size of a thumb on the column. It is believed that if you can stick your thumb into it and turn your hand clockwise one full circle with fingers open, then your wish will come true. Everyone was taking a chance. Nicholas joined the queue and made a wish. The hole in the column was fairly humid. He continued pacing thinking, "this is why they must have called it the sweating column".

The temple offered a different view from each corner. It was a place with a strange and curious atmosphere.

As he walked, Nicholas noticed comparatively smaller locked doors on the interior side walls. It was widely rumored among the people of the time that Architect Fossati who conducted the last repair of the temple during the latter period of the Ottomans, had some doors covered hidden. For this reason, Nicholas was searching for a sign, a covered door.

To the left of the main entrance, there was a section leading to the second floor. Nicholas headed there. There weren't any customary stairs. A gentle stone floored spiral path climbed to the upper section. Together with a tourist group, Nicholas walked spiraling to the upper floor with slow steps. It was a fairly bright area closer to the windows. Ceiling decorations and fine masonry workmanship of the columns were more visible. Temple looked much different from the upper floor. The details of the dome and the angelic figurines were more noticeable. The Jesus frescoes on the second floor walls were magnificent. Nicholas was mixed with feelings. Here was a striking spiritual ambiance.

He headed back to the main floor below. Continued pacing inside the building with slow steps. Floors were covered with massive marble panes. In front of the temple were additions constructed during the Ottomans. These were add-ons such as pulpit and altar indicating the direction of Mecca which is present in all Muslim mosques. Nicholas thought that these fine workmanship add-ons integrated beautifully with the temple ornamentation and enriched the space instead of distorting it. Muslims visiting the temple were not disturbed by the angelic dome figurines which were not actually compatible with their beliefs, and the Christians didn't seem to be offended by these add-ons. It was as if all religions had become a whole here. This place was nothing like any other churches. Here it felt like the common spirit of the humanity walked about. Temple seemed to house brotherhood.

It was like Jerusalem incident all over again. He thought he would find something on the first day of his arrival. He thought important events would take place before nightfall. But he had walked for twenty seven days on the streets of Jerusalem in search of a sign. It was only the seventh day of his arrival in Istanbul. Every morning he had his breakfast at the hotel terrace watching the Bosphorus, Hagia Sophia and unequalled scenery of the city and walked only a few hundred yards to the temple, and spent his entire day there.

The summer heat was beginning to be felt in the city. After breakfast, Nicholas headed for Hagia Sophia. He always felt a sweet peace the moment he entered the temple, as if he had arrived home. As usual he walked directly to the spot beneath the exact center of the dome, the point where he dreamt about the Man Carrying Water. This spot was the exact center of the temple and the dome. Gazing at the dome above from that point was visually intoxicating. This spot gave Nicholas an inexplicable excitement. He was looking at the dome right above him with his neck streched back with a sincere wish thinking, "It was right here in my dream. Please God, let me see a sign"...

"Sir, are you alright?" were the words which suddenly stripped him from all his thoughts. The security guard was in front of him. Nicholas was looking at him surprised and confused. Guard was saying "for more than hour you've been stuck here standing, are you alright, are you well?" He didn't know how to respond, but was finally able to say "I am sorry, I was just immersed in my memories", and slowly moved on.

He looked at his watch, it was true, he had been just standing there in the middle of Hagia Sophia for more than an hour. Confused and in deep thoughts, Nicholas walked about but the security guard was not too far behind. Although the guard was very careful not to disturb this curious visitor; nevertheless, he kept an eye on him from a fair distance. Not surprising. After all, this was first a church, later a mosque and then became a museum many years ago.

Security was highly sensitive and it was almost the end of the visiting hours. He thought "a warm shower and rest at the hotel" and headed in that direction.

He preferred to have dinner in his room after a warm shower. He ordered the famous Turkish kebab from the hotel restaurant. Food was excellent. The terrific scenery made it even more pleasant. After dinner he began reading the information he had gathered about Hagia Sophia.

Until late hours of the night he read and sipped Turkish coffee watching Hagia Sophia from his balcony. Later he couldn't resist exhaustion anymore and fell asleep with his mind absorbed in thoughts. Waking up in full view of Hagia Sophia gave him a distinct pleasure. But today was a little different. It was the month of June and beginning of the summer, but the sky was covered with rain clouds and so it was a little depressing. He quickly took a shower and went to the hotel terrace on the top floor for a breakfast. This was the place he enjoyed most in the hotel. It was covered with glass all around and had incredible panoramic view. Magnificent scenery of Istanbul was in full view. On one side the Bosphorus which separated two continents and joined two seas, the high Galata Tower although at a distance, and on the other side Hagia Sophia standing magnificently beside him with all of its grandeur, and a little further down, Sultanahmet's renowned giant Blue Mosque with its six very high minarets.... It couldn't get any better. It was impossible to put into words. Having breakfast in view of this wonderful scenery was indescribable. Starting the day like this energized him.

Rain clouds gathered even more as time went by... This weather gave a unique beauty to Hagia Sophia and the Bosphorus... Nicholas grabbed a cup of tea and headed to his room. Drinking tea at his balcony while looking at Hagia Sophia had become a newly discovered pleasure and a tradition for him. Perhaps due to the encounter with the security guard the day before, or perhaps due to discouragement of seeing no signs of any kind in the temple or the threat of rain, he thought "Today I will stay in. The view is amazing." He placed his tea cup on the balcony table, carefully took out the "Book of Secrets" from the case, sat at the table and read again the writing on the first page. Turned over the second page. He was looking at the large writing "Water" and trying to resolve what it meant...

Before going to bed the previous night, he had taken the foolish risk and sprinkled a couple of drops on several pages hoping for new signs. Nothing happened and he regretted his foolishness. Only the writing which had appeared before were there. He kept sipping his delicious Turkish tea thinking, "The inscription WATER covering the pages is trying to say something, but what?"

■■

Nicholas took refuge in the pleasure of a cup of tea in sight of Hagia Sophia which he dreamt repeatedly, the mysterious book he uncovered at Mount Olive through a map given to him by a man dying and numerous unanswered questions.

The gentle breeze had brought a couple of droplets to his face, the first signs of rain coming. The breeze and the aroma of rain coming was very sweet. Droplets gathered speed. Hagia Sophia took on a different appearance under rain. While watching the view in wonderment, he suddenly felt a small brilliant ray next to him. With a sudden reflex he looked at the table.

His eyes remained fixed at the "Book of Secrets" on the table. On the page there were several sparks resembling but weaker than the shimmering which had happened in his Jerusalem hotel room. After every droplet the page shimmered, dissipated and a letter was formed. What happened on the page was incomprehensible. His eyes just remained stuck. Quickly pulled himself together when the shimmering stopped. Turned another page and captured a few more droplets, with each droplet the same thing kept happening, sparkling and shimmering continued, letters kept forming and all stopped. Turned over all the pages one by one under the rain droplets. Nothing happened. Only three pages showed new inscriptions. He was soaking wet in the balcony. His heart was beating furiously with joy. Entered his room with excitement. He was soaked but he didn't care. He placed the book on the table and began reading:

■■■

"If this page became legible, you either met him or you are very lucky and opened the book under rain. If you are reading this book under rain, then I am sorry because you won't be able to read any more pages other than these. In order to be able to read them, you must find Him. I wish you a long journey with Him. Mine was very short."
■■■

He was able to read the writings easily. The inscription continued, but although readable, they were a bunch of incomprehensible words. Nicholas began wondering and kept asking, "Which language is this?" Suddenly he recalled that Da Vinci had a habit of ciphering the words by writing in reverse and from right to left. He had read this information in an old book at a library in Rome. Immediately stepped in front of his room mirror and reflected the page off the mirror. Yes, now it was readable:

"Behold Leonardo. Do not question or oppose Him, otherwise the journey will end. For humanity's sake, try keeping your journey long. Man Carrying a Water Jug holds all the secrets. Beware, He has no shadow under the sun. He is shadowless... But, the secret of Man Carrying a Water Jug is that clay jug which he never puts aside."

■■■

Nicholas flipped gently to the next page and kept reading in amazement and awe...

"I, Leonardo. The Man Carrying a Water Jug told me a few things about women. But these were totally contrary to my religious doctrine. The first night it was mentioned, we were in Zeugma. We were in a house on a slope facing the River Euphrates. The floor mosaic had wonderful pictures. These were pictures depicting a mythological event.

I was so affected by what the Man Carrying a Water Jug had said to me about women, I was ready to fall in love with the first woman I would see on the street and kiss her feet. Even the mosaic figurine of the woman on the floor gave me pleasure with what had been told to me. That night, I Leonardo made a painting of a woman looking at that mosaic picture. I called it Mona Lisa."

Nicholas gently flipped to the next page in anxious excitement. This page, too, had a short inscription formed on it. Swallowing his breath, he read it at once:

"Behold, Leonardo. The Man Carrying a Water Jug who gave me amazing secrets and enabled me to make discoveries cut my journey short because of the objections I raised about women and many questions I asked. We met only ten times in six months. I wish the journey hadn't ended..."

Her sorrowful face, dreamy gaze with a thousand tales, the Gypsy Girl with mysterious look made anyone who glimpsed at her fall in love with her at once. Her not so neat hair, protruding cheekbones, and firm full face were ravishing. People wondered asking, "Who might she be?" They peeked at her at length from varying angles as if they were memorizing her sight.

Nicholas was among those looking at the Gypsy Girl in adoration. Their eyes were meeting. The Gypsy Girl was applying this thing called the eye contact. Whether he was in motion or at a remote corner, the eye contact remained intact. The Gypsy Girl did not lose her eye contact. It was as if she was casting a spell on everyone there looking at her.

Nicholas thinking, "No, this is not the mosaic I am looking for, but this is weird" while lightly stroking his chin also wanted to see the other mosaics, but couldn't abandon the mosaic portrait called the "Gypsy Girl".

After the Leonarda Da Vinci confessions appearing on the book pages under rain and having spent a sleepless and anxious night in front of his computer, and learning that the Zeugma mentioned in the Da Vinci's 'Book of Secrets' was a city of antiquity in Turkey near the river Euphrates, and that the mosaics found in the halls and rooms during archeological digs of magnificent villas facing the river were being exhibited at the Gaziantep Zeugma Mosaic Museum, he arrived at Gaziantep with the first flight available early in the morning.

The place he was standing in was the exhibit hall on the second floor of the museum where the "Gypsy Girl" was on a specially arranged display. He had seen numerous mosaic pictures in the first floor. They were all uniquely wonderful. And he had been in this special section on the second floor for more than half an hour. The mosaic was created with such an incredible mastery of art that regardless from where you look at the picture, the eyes of the woman in the mosaic did not lose her eye contact with you.

The museum guides were explaining that the reason for calling her the "Gypsy Girl" was that all other mosaics in the exhibit had names and epithets, but only this one was nameless, and so the archeologists gave her this name because of her braiding. It was impossible not to be affected with the mastery of art in eyes following and not adore the mosaic.

Nicholas tried many times to view the picture from different directions but the eye contact was there wherever he stood. Whether you walk fast or move slowly the "Gypsy Girl" followed you with her eyes. It was obvious that an unbelievable technique had been used in creating the mosaic. Talking in his own mind again saying, "This is not the picture Da Vinci is talking about, but there is something here", Nicholas slowly approached the mosaic closer. The hall was filled with curious tourists. While he was silently observing the picture the people to the side drew his attention. Fairly loud and comfortable, they were conversing about the mosaic. Their focus, posture and stance suggested that they were professionals with expertise. The one slightly overweight was saying to the other, "The most important element which makes it interesting is the care and mysterious mastery used in placement of the eye pupils. Regardless of from where you look at it, the female figure in the panel looks at you continuously with a 360 degree angle from top to bottom and from right to left. She never separates her eyes from the onlooker."

Nicholas was hearing them clearly since he was near them. He wasn't too engaged with what was being said. Just as he readied himself to depart with the thought, "I better find the mosaic which modeled for Mona Lisa painting" and stepped back, he was frozen stiff when he heard one of the art experts say, "My friend, we see this eye-following qualities in Leonardo Da Vinci's Mona Lisa painting as well as his painting called 'La Jakond'".

The words changed Nicholas' mind. He stayed. The conversation was going on and the man said, "If it weren't for the 1300 and odd years difference, I would have said this mosaic and the Mona Lisa painting belonged to the same person because the identical technique used".

As if he had resolved the mystery, Nicholas was now looking at the picture with more intent and care under the effect of the words he had just heard. He thought, "Da Vinci must have been influenced by this technique and used it in the Mona Lisa drawing."

There must have been another mosaic where this painting was unearthed. Because Da Vinci was saying that he had made the Mona Lisa painting under the influence of what the Man Carrying a Water Jug had said about women in a house in Zeugma and by looking at a mosaic female figure.

Nicholas began walking from mosaic to mosaic in the museum. It was as if most of the mosaics depicted legends. Snakes, angels, strange creatures... Da Vinci had also said in his 'Book of Secrets' that "the mosaics on the floor were wonderful pictures telling a mythological event."

Suddenly Nicholas moved toward a mosaic with an uncontrolled reflex. He had moved too fast toward the picture. In an urge, just as he was about to touch it, he came to his senses with the warning of a museum official who said, "Please, do not touch the mosaics". He quickly pulled back and began looking at it anxiously.

It was obvious that picture was telling a mythological story. There were fish figurines of various sizes. The edges of the mosaic were decorated like a photograph frame. A nude man riding a strange creature similar to a fish was being shown. It was clear that it was depicted as an angel. In the mid section of the mosaic a male head with vigorous hair was seen. This reminded Nicholas of Zeus from the Greek mythology. Immediately adjacent to this man was the woman figure which excited Nicholas and pulled him toward the mosaic. Nicholas was whispering to himself in excitement... "Clearly this must be Mona Lisa."

Definitely, the woman figure depicted immediately adjacent to what could be interpreted as a male god was the picture of Mona Lisa. The only difference was that this woman had eyebrows. Da Vinci was clearly saying he had drawn Mona Lisa after being influenced what the Man Carrying a Water Jug had said about women. The model was this mosaic figure. It was a reflection of Da Vinci's state of mind with what was told about women, perhaps the absence of eyebrows was an irony. Did he not say "what he told me about women was conflicting with my religious knowledge" and thus implied it.

Catching a glimpse of Hagia Sophia again when he opened his eyes to the ring of telephone gave him a strange joy. Slowly reached at the phone which was still ringing. With a pleasant voice the receptionist woman was saying excitedly, "Good morning sir, your friend from America is on the line. He says he couldn't reach you on your mobile. All day long yesterday and last night he called you multiple times. He seemed to be quite worried. We, too, were worried when we couldn't reach you. Thank God you came this morning".

With a tired voice Nicholas responded, "Thank you very much for your concern. There is nothing to worry about".

"I am connecting you now, sir."

On the other end of the line Michael who was clearly worried jumped on him with a seriously concerned voice, "Thank God you're alive, buddy. Are you OK? Somethin's the matter with you? Why the hell's your mobile off line? Dam'it Nicko, what the hell's goin' on?"

Still half awake and drowsy, little agitated, Nicholas interjected. Otherwise the endless questioning would have gone on, "Cool down, cool down Mikey. Nothin' to worry pal... I'm fine, buddy. There's nothin' wrong". Feeling tired, Nicholas quickly rose from his bed and moved on to the table.

"You know, that...aaa... you know, that 'Book of Secrets' I found in Jerusalem ..."

This time Michael interrupted forcefully. Obviously he was much stressed and still fearful for having failed to contact Nicholas on numerous occasions: "Well, what happen'd to it? Someone's trailing you?"

Now a little more awake, "No, no... Of course not... nobody's trailin' me, buddy... Where the hell you're gettin' these ideas? Calm down, will you? Incredible things are happening, don't worry... New writings appeared on the book pages with rain droplets. There are confessions from Leonardo Da Vinci."

Clearly shocked, Michael repeated, "What... confessions?" but obviously his mind was still focused elsewhere, and he carried on as usual, "...leave the friggin book and Leonard alone, will you... tell me where the hell you've been.."

Nicholas felt guilty for having neglected his only trusted soul and knew it was time to provide some explanation, "Believe me, bro.. there is nothin' to worry.. Some new writings appeared in the book. Da Vinci was talking about things at a place called Zeugma, things like…aa… mosaics. This…aa…Zeugma is an archeological city here in Turkey. The mosaics dug out were apparently on exhibit in a museum... I went to see them... It was a momentary travel decision. My mobile charge ran out by the time I got there. I couldn't schedule my return and ended up spending a night there, took the first flight out and now I am here. Receptionists told me you had called, I was gonna get back to you. It seems I've collapsed and fell asleep. It's been a thriller and very exhausting...

I'm really sorry, buddy... My mobile is still dead... I'll plug it in now..."

As if to suggest being a little comforted with the words heard, Michael said, "OK, at least I now know nothin's happened to you, I'm very glad... but buddy... be careful... leave this business alone..Don't let this weird deal get you into trouble... Look, like Opus Dei, Knights of the Temple, Templars, masons, friggin' outfits... friggin' shady characters... you never know... you know what I mean... Trouble we don't need... Come back already... and if this book is really Da Vinci's, it will be worth millions... Believe me, I know, I heard... an influential businessman paid millions for sketches of Leonardo done for a bridge and some buildings in Istanbul..."

There was a momentary silence. Things he was hearing were always on the back of Nicholas' mind. Although he appeared to be carrying on decisively, lately he was making abrupt choices, and doubts were gnawing his brain along the way... "You're right, buddy... I wanna say I want to return right away, but I'm gonna stay a little more... I can feel it, shortly something's gonna happen here in Istanbul... My dreams disappear here... In Jerusalem I was dreamin' every damn night... But here, not even once... Last night I had to stay in Gaziantep and had the same dream... It disappears only here near Hagia Sophia…"

Nicholas' last words were clearly indicating that he was determined to carry on with this adventure, Michael, as if to show his displeasure, and with a disappointed tone of voice said, "OK, buddy... you know best... but be careful, will you?"

In an attempt to comfort his friend Nicholas replied, "Do not worry… If strange things begin to happen… If I feel any danger at all… I'll return immediately…"

"OK, buddy, I'll be waitin'... Well, what did you do... did you find anything?"

While he began answering, "I just mentioned it, didn't I? Well... the rain droplets on the pages...", Michael on the other end interrupted, "I'm not talkin' about that pal... What I mean is did you figure out a slogan? There are only three weeks left for the presentation... Are you aware of this?"

Michael's words were calling out Nicholas from the world of secrets and mysteries, to the reality of life in New York. Not having gotten a quick response from Nicholas, Michael kept talking... "Look, bro... Even though I nearly cracked up here with worry and lost my sleep worryin' about you, I didn't wanna bother you as we agreed... You only dropped a few lines of e-mail... OK, you did mention leaving Jerusalem for Istanbul, hotel phone numbers, what's been happenin' with the book... But not a single word on what really matters... Only three weeks to the presentation... I thought you might have found a slogan already, so I had to call you yesterday... Well, your mobile was off, and you weren't at the hotel last night... I got worried, buddy, what do you expect?"

Hoping to calm down his friend Nicholas said, "I know, I understand... I'm not about to blame you for breaking our rules..."

Nicholas and Michael had among them an unwritten business rule. During the process of creating a new slogan and advertisement for a client company, Michael stayed at the office and Nicholas removed himself from everything for several weeks. During this time they tried to produce striking messages. They had an agreement not to be in touch unless Nicholas called first. Days later, whenever Nicholas would return to the office with new ideas and bursting energy, they would celebrate it like a festivity, and after a final brain-storming, they would go on with their client presentations. These rules began surfacing during the university years while they were working as interns at that famous advertising company, but firmed up when they started their own company. The advertising adventure of Nicholas which began during his internship helped him rise to the creative group within a short period, and having attracted the attention of the upper management, he became head of the creative group and continued as the lead writer. They referred to him as the 'golden boy' of the advertising world. His self-confidence had peaked every time the advertising company rewarded Nicholas with salary increases, gifts and vacations after every successful campaign. Subsequently, he had developed a different style and trusted affiliations with corporate clients, and entered into a unique realm of advertising with knowledge and information acquired about personalities and businesses. He was consulted by corporate heads and he provided striking advice to them. His commentary to some clients such as "do not spend advertising money for this product, it won't sell in the market, I recommend you concentrate on another type of product" caused discomfort among the upper management of this renowned advertising company. This discomfort was not made obvious to Nicholas. The main reason was that the giant energy drink corporate client of the firm was entirely captivated by Nicholas. This client was an average energy drink company when they had first came to the advertising firm asking, "find for us a striking slogan, we want our product to be popular with our ads on TV". At that time disregarding the objections of the creative group, and using his authority as the group leader, Nicholas made a presentation to the drink company's management. With Nicholas' suggestion to obtain extreme sports sponsorships in various countries around the world, competition series, shows, and a presentation crowned with an incredible slogan motivated the client company management who had previously considered only a strong entry to the US market became a global player in an instant. The advertising firm acquired a client which was dubbed a 'big fish'. Business exceeded expectations; the drink company became a successful global leader and made enormous advertising payments. This created a golden age for Nicholas within the firm. Vice-presidency at such young age was an unbelievable success.

But, the genius of effective slogans and advertising scripts was also responsible for unacquired accounts and lost clients. Lately, the list was getting long, the yogurt manufacturer who got slapped with, "come back to us after removing unhealthy ingredients", the drinking water company who got kicked with, "sell your water in non-cancerogen quality plastic bottles, better yet, use a glass bottle", the shampoo corporation who was defied with, "this ingredient in your shampoo makes cancer, remove it and use a harmless ingredient..." The upper management of the advertising firm was very uncomfortable. They had numerous meetings with Nicholas, but these were meetings always concluded with the statement "public health is none of your business, your job is to find slogans and sell their products..."

Despite such occasional unpleasantries he continued working sincerely, but one day he resigned unexpectedly. Without any hesitation. The energy drink company had wanted to discuss a matter over dinner at a very reputable restaurant. He had gone to the business dinner meeting thinking it would be like those previous pleasant ones, but he resigned from vice-presidency the next morning. One sentence brought the resignation, "Your firm is asking us questions such as 'will you continue to work with us if Nicholas is not with us?' and is conducting persuasion meetings".

His resignation news shook the advertising circles and invitations flooded from other companies. Nicholas did the unexpected. With is buddy Michael who also resigned at the same time, they jointly established a new company called 'Daimon Investment Consultancy and Advertising". Their first client was the energy drink company which severed its ties with their former employer. This enabled them to make a smooth transition. But they knew they needed new clients for sound business. However, whenever Nicholas identified an unfair situation, he would object immediately and create a difficult process. Finally, a tooth paste product company which met Nicholas' approval excited Michael. When Nicholas had established through a lab examination that the product contained a very useful ingredient for teeth health and said "we need to find an incredible slogan for this", then for Michael, a new miracle in the horizon appeared. At the time when Michael was excited and working on the project, that mysterious elderly man who introduced himself as a museum director came to their new office, and after the phone conversation with Nicholas informing him of this odd situation, the Jerusalem adventure began. Michael was vehemently in favor of acquiring this client which he considered a 'big fish'. But, even if he hated the thought of it, he just couldn't say to his only buddy, "this is important business opportunity, do not go to Jerusalem". In any event, Nicholas had said at the airport on his way to Jerusalem "Don't worry, I would have gone somewhere for finding a slogan any way, I will look around a little, find incredible slogans and everyone will buy our tooth-paste".

Although Michael was worried day in and day out, he hesitated to call him due to unwritten rules. But, he had to make that call not only because he dearly cared for this money-making opportunity, but also there were only a few short weeks left till the presentation.

The short silence was broken with Michael's hopeless voice, "We can't let these guys go. Buddy, you've found one hell of a time to chase after this dream. We got to get these guys. These guys are the big fish. We need this account. You know this better than me…"

Nicholas' voice came through more confidently on the subject, "The slogan is ready pal, don't worry. Not only that, I got a terrific tooth-brush idea for them. If we can convince them, the two products will be super complement for each other, as far as I'm concerned, it is not only the tooth-paste, it's also the brush..."

Michael who couldn't hide his joy was yelling on the line, "that's it, that's it buddy... This is it... My man, my man… You are terrific. Incredible. I'm with you all the way!"

Michael was very pleased with the news. But still he hadn't given up, as if to demonstrate his serious doubts he kept saying, "…look bro, I'm saying this again, Da Vinci is a man with weird secrets... Everyone says he has weird friggin' messages in his art. Lots of shady characters and organizations are after the Holy Grail. Why don't you take some time off, c'mon back right away, will you?"

Slow, indecisive and staggering sentences dropped out of Nicholas' lips while he was seated and gazing at the Hagia Sophia: "I really don't know how to explain this, bro… But as far as I can make out of it… Da Vinci had spoken with the Man Carrying a Water Jug… You know those hidden messages in his paintings, you know, The last Dinner, Mona Lisa and the others..."

Confused, Michael interrupted, "Wait a minute, will you? Hold on... How could two people who lived in different centuries have possibly spoken with one another? Are you sure, buddy? You know what you're talkin' bout?…"

"I dont know… Da Vinci is saying that in his confessions in the book... I agree there is something weird goin' on…" What Nicholas was implying that new mysteries were added to the ones he couldn't resolve yet...

When Michael retorted, "Why don't you bring the book here right away? There are experts here... Let's talk to them...", his real intention was to help his friend and convince him to return at once to his home.

Nicholas kept on talking without being responsive to his friend's words, "OK, there could be ciphered messages in those paintings, but what's really important is that these paintings are hiding secrets. I think there are secrets either he couldn't accept or those he was unable to reveal. Paintings have secretive meanings beyond simple ciphers".

Even though he couldn't grasp exactly what Nicholas was trying to explain, still wanting to be persuasive, Michael insisted without being blunt, "OK, I understand, there are complicated things... Just come back... Like I said... We will talk to the professors... A little break will be good for you... and... aa... we will also catch the big fish in the meantime..."

"OK... OK, there is just a little more left. I can feel something's about to happen... But I promise... I'll be in the States before the meeting."

Firmness of the words made Michael feel that Nicholas was not about to leave this adventure. He knew him all too well... Aware of the futility of insistence, Michael said, "OK, buddy, please take good care. You never know... don't fall for a covered black head to heel, will you? You might end up there with a harem of your own... We don't wanna loose you... got it?" With his catchy laughter resembling that of cartoon film characters, he had Nicholas laughing also regardless of all that distance in between... It didn't matter, anyone would get caught in Michael's laughter.

"Bro, you know something, films don't tell the truth. Life in Istanbul and people's clothing are just like those in New York. The only difference is the historical structures which have been standing here for centuries. People are just like us... Their lives and families are just like ours..." It was as if Nicholas was trying to correct an injustice done...

Michael softly responded, "interesting situation.. Let's get this new account and I, too, will visit Istanbul. I await your return enthusiastically. I am saying again… take good care of yourself… Call me once in a while… Remember you are not only after an adventure. You are also engaged in an ad business process… Soften our rules a little… I really get worried… you know…" Michael was clearly indicating that he didn't need any headaches, worries and troubles…

Nicholas chuckled a little and said, "OK… I'll call you, but rules not too loose, alright?" and added "you take care also… Let me take a shower and we'll talk again". Nicholas slowly placed back the handset of the phone after Michael's words, "God bless you"…

There was a large crowd in front of Hagia Sophia again. Tourist groups from everywhere were waiting in line. After a long wait, he was able to enter the temple. He felt a momentary peace as if he had arrived home. In a reflex he headed toward the area exactly beneath the dome. This had almost become a habit for him. Whenever he came to the temple, he headed there immediately, perhaps with a hope and expectation within, exactly to the spot he dreamt below the center of the dome…

He had taken a warm shower after his phone conversation with Michael and as usual enjoyed his breakfast at the top floor of his hotel in full view of the magnificent scenery, and with a strange peace in him, he walked quickly to Hagia Sophia.

As he neared the area beneath the dome, he saw a young woman standing still at the center with her eyes focused at the dome, with her chin fully raised. Strong rays of sun were beaming through the windows high up. Two separate beams from the top right and left windows were merging and hitting the central spot. Her face uplifted and invisible to Nicholas, a girl was standing there. With her shoulder length golden hair, thin and erect graceful body, she resembled a goddess with her chin-up figure in the light of sun rays. Nicholas was mesmerized, incapable of any thought. When she lowered her head a few moments later, their gazes interlocked. Her smile was very warm. Their eyes were glued in silence for a fraction of time that seemed like eternity. Nicholas was lost in those blue eyes. This inexplicable magical moment of two strangers locked in gaze was suddenly interrupted by another woman saying, "Come on Kristen, let's see the upper floor" and dragging her hand. Both women were in their twenties. Nicholas' gaze was frozen with sudden turbulent storms breaking inside him. Without realizing his purpose and in full daze, he began walking after them. In loss of control, he was now stalking her as if she had put on a spell on him. His only desire was to keep alive his intoxicated senses and remain buried in her attraction. Initially the girl didn't notice anything. But the perky, graceful woman was not late in noticing the young man tracking her... When she turned back for a full glimpse, they came eye to eye once again. Nicholas was helpless, didn't know what to do or say. At that very moment his entire body shook, he almost fell flat on his face. He did not realize exactly how and when they reached the upper floor after walking the spiral climb. In the left section marble flooring, the central part was slightly sunken. Under her spell, he hadn't noticed this and Nicholas found himself on the floor while still locked in her eyes. Somewhat embarrassed, he made an attempt to rise and met those spell-binding blue eyes pleasantly asking, "Are you, OK?" Nicholas couldn't utter a word. Either because of the embarrassment of the fall or the storm created in his heart by the girl he had met moments ago, speechless he was stuck in a pair of eyes, it was as if he had been lost in a blue ocean...

He reached out reluctantly to the hand extended by her. Nicholas was like an innocent child under the spell of a sweet enchantress. He was focused at her, but only to the void in her pupils as if wanting to discover himself in them. He felt an incredibly pleasant sensation in his entire body the moment their hands touched. A feeling of eternal unity arose in him with this initial touch.

Her hands were cotton soft. He arose in embarrassment and clumsily began dusting off his pants. The other woman had lost her control over her suppressed smile and was now giggling annoyingly. In further embarrassment, Nicholas was finally able to say, "didn't see it coming, I was absorbed with the beauty of the place, couldn't notice the dent". As if wanting to calm Nicholas, she replied, "...the temple is very beautiful, one can't notice the floor while looking above, that's what I've been doing also..." The other girl still giggling said "Really! I too was looking up... and guess what I saw..." and burst into laughter. "My cousin is always like this, footloose, happy–go–lucky. She laughs all the time. Don't take it personally... By the way, I am Kristen..." were the words of the girl who spell-bound Nicholas.

Nicholas extended his hand, but while he was saying, "I'm Nicholas. Pleased to meet you," the feel of her hand blurred his mind pleasantly. Hand shaking continued for just another sweet moment until the other interrupted with her hand reaching forward and still giggling, "Hi, I'm Amber".

Nicholas, reluctant to lose the feel of Kristen's touch, let go of her hand and shook Amber's hand saying, "Happy to meet you", and a little shy, added "Just didn't see it coming, I was... examining the temple..." Amber burst into laughter again saying with a little devilish hint, "That was a nice fall..." Nicholas was unable to salvage the situation, but he really didn't care too much either. He was under the influence of an incredible sensation. While looking into Kristen's eyes, he really did hear neither Amber nor the humming of the tourists around.

Amber was still laughing when Kristen handed over the camera saying, "Well, if no trouble, will you please take a photo of us?".

Even if Kristen issued a warning with gentle voice saying, "Stop it, it's not fair", her cousin's giggling continued with a response "…can't help it, what can I do?"

Nicholas said, "with pleasure…" and took the camera. Now an incredible view was in his sight, the magnificent Hagia Sophia and Kristen.

The photographing ritual which began on the second floor of Hagia Sophia continued to the remote corners of the temple in warm, friendly and sincere chat as if they had known each other for years. It was either single shots or camera shots of the duet. In photos jointly with Kristen, Nicholas was happy with a child's innocence.

While in pure and youthful joy of taking photographs in Hagia Sophia, they discovered in their chats that they had much in common. Just as Nicholas, Kristen and Amber were also New York residents. Amber was a nurse. Kristen was studying at the School of Visual Arts in New York.

Three New Yorkers had met at an ancient temple thousands of miles away from their home. Although it seemed as if the familiarity of being fellow townspeople and of the same nationality had initiated a warm communication among them, an unspoken, silent, mind intoxicating dialogue which began in the eyes through the hearts was established between Nicholas and Kristen. A storm which erupted in the hearts with a little smile and a single eye contact… That gaze and that smile… What else could have possibly given this sweet high other than this gaze and smile? Nicholas was still mesmerized and had difficulty in grasping what was being said. Kristen's voice was echoing like a sweet melody in his mind.

On numerous occasions his close friends in New York had introduced and set up Nicholas with their friends. But he had repeatedly indicated his unwillingness saying, "Please, don't do this again, will you?" When Nicholas spoke about relationships with his friends, in particular with Michael, they couldn't say much in opposing arguments. Especially against the glitter in Nicholas' eyes when he repeated the word "love"...

When his friends pressed him on the subject, as if to express his high expectations from love, Nicholas would be quick to retort, "Do you think what we experience is really 'love'? What goes on today is not 'love' when compared to the past, it is merely an animalistic coupling with all of its material aspects, irrationalities and temporary lust. In today's disenchanted and broken life, there is no divine poetry of love or any bewildering magic... Today, love has covered the streets... in front of our eyes... spreading like bush fire with no shame and hesitation... as if on a theatrical stage... There are men and women who engage multiple lovers in a typical day... There are women, aren't there, with breasts naked to the crevices, in parties and gatherings... We encounter hundreds of them... We can engage them in any subject, divulge anything... and they are more aggressive and obsessive than we are... Women are loosing their real magnetism caused by inviting aloofness, impossibility of easy access and challenge of trust. With women in this state, love has become an ordinary item of commerce, and its eternal joy was subjugated to immediate material gain... Excitement, doubts, fear, and those poems, and the poetry of it all are long lost..."

But, Kristen now had done with one innocent sincere smile of eyes all that his fiends failed to do.

While looking from the upper floor of Hagia Sophia at the people below and with brief, intermittent adoring glimpses at Kristen near him, he recalled the magic words he had read in a Vatican library and kept repeating all these years, now storming his heart:

"It is mentioned in the ancient Sanskrit legends that love is fated, and preordained souls are destined to meet. According to the same legends, the person is immediately recognized, you will know and enjoy every transition in motion, thought, moment and feelings expressed in the eyes. It is said that we recognize them by their wings. These are wings only visible to the lover. And the love for that person diminishes all our other desires."

Nicholas was seeing Kristen's wings. Those magnificent wings invisible to all others...

Amber was pointing at her watch saying "Guys we have been at it for three hours, are you aware of it?" Has it been that long really? Nicholas and Kristen looked at each other in amazement. Amber carried on saying, "...don't know about you, but I'm famished to the edge of collapse". Nicholas jumped at it and extended a sincere invitation to the girls, "My hotel is a hundred yards away, the restaurant on the top floor has a terrific view of the city. You must see it, the Turkish cuisine is full of surprising delights". The offer of wonderful city scenery following a warm dialogue was impossible to decline.

They were now at the restaurant after a short and pleasant conversation filled fast paced walk. Kristen kept repeating her feelings of adoration with her eyes on the city, "...can't believe this. This is incredible...This can't be real, it's so beautiful..."

They ordered the famed Turkish *kebab* from the hotel's menu. The spectacular panorama of the city quickly impressed the girls. Amber was already busy taking photos. She was impatient to upload the photos to her Facebook page and kept repeating, "what an incredible view, everyone's gonna luv' it". While Amber was a happy-go-lucky fun girl, Kristen was nearly the opposite, mature and calm girl. There was trace of nobility hidden in her every move. Try as hard as he may, Nicholas couldn't help looking at Kristen in admiration.

A little while later the kebabs arrived like ornaments to their table and they ate in pleasant conversation accompanying Amber's interruptions claiming, "This is unbelievable, very delicious". Although Amber appeared to be carrying on the conversation, in reality Kristen and Nicholas were conversing with intoxicating eye contacts.

Suddenly Amber burst into laughter again saying, "I wish you had dropped on us earlier, we could have gone around and maybe see interesting places together, we didn't see anything like this since our arrival". She was having difficulty carrying on, but embarrassed Nicholas by saying, "you dropping on us was really cool". He was embarrassed and did not say a word, but just smiled. He had smiled with a reflex because Amber was in giggles, actually he was nearly unaware of what she was saying. He was in a world of tales walking with an angel. "I wish we didn't have to leave tomorrow night…" Amber's words struck the dreamy world of Nicholas like a thunderbolt. In a sad tone, all he could say was "Are you leaving?" "Unfortunately… The exhibit ended today… We are returning to New York tomorrow night…", these words of Kristen gave him intense agony at that very moment. As if making fun, Amber again in a sly tone added, "look at the guy, he is feeling sorry… You aren't gonna stay here forever, are you? Like he isn't coming back to New York..." All three felt comforted, Amber's words were an open invitation to continue the affair in New York. They had indeed met just a few hours ago, but it did feel as if they had known each other for several years.

A little discrete, Kristen said, "I need to go back to the museum, I need to help my friends. We came here for our school exhibit at the Pera Museum. We need to pack the paintings and artifacts. I am already so late." These words were like the classical exit of a fairy stepping out of a hopeless romance, a dreamy theatrical stage on which Nicholas was the lover being abandoned. They exchanged phone numbers like a ritual with an unknown outcome. While Nicholas accompanied them to the hotel exit, he found the courage to say, "Well, if you are leaving tomorrow night, what about turning the city upside down during the day? There are many places to see…" Girls glimpsed at each other silently smiling. This time Kristen jumped in, "OK, but this time food is on us" and these words made Nicholas walk on air. At the very moment girls took a corner waving hands and disappeared from the end of the narrow old Istanbul street while he was almost jumping in happiness and wouldn't have cared if he had shouted amongst the pedestrians with excitement.

It was a long night for Nicholas and the morning refused to arrive. He couldn't sleep and kept calculating what he could do to further impress Kristen. He kept stepping out to the balcony looking at the Hagia Sophia, reentering his room and stealing a glimpse of the 'Book of Secrets' but not a single thought concerning these past events drew his attention. Neither the Man Carrying a Water Jug seen to him in his dream at Hagia Sophia, nor the "WATER" noted in all the pages of the 'Book of Secrets' mattered. Tonight it was only Kristen whose pictures flipped one after another on the computer screen...

He was spellbound and kept seeing her wherever he looked, even when his eyes were closed. It was as if the pictures were not flowing on the screen, but in the labyrinth of his mind. She was everywhere smiling. Life felt like gaining a new meaning. He felt joy to his guts all the way to his bones.

The hotel room eventually became claustrophobic. It was fairly late into the night. He was fully awake. He wanted to go out and run like mad, scream his heart out. He felt he could do this, had it not been so late in the night but the streets looked empty, silent and abandoned. He hesitated to step out. Grabbed his laptop and went up to the terrace. It was spacious and refreshing. Asked for a cup of mid-sweet Turkish coffee with a cold glass of water on the side. He learned this manner of coffee ritual by observing the Turks and from the helpful waiter who always welcomed him warmly with a sincere and honest smile. The delicious flavor of the specially prepared not too sweet coffee was to be washed down with cool sips of pure spring water. He wished he could share this with Kristen. Instead, Kristen's photos were on the screen, the magnificent Hagia Sophia spot-lit cleverly just beside him with its awesome silent presence and wisdom of ages, and of course the jewel-like glittering lights of endless Istanbul, an ancient and still modern city....

He suddenly stood up. He looked at the panorama and the picture on the screen, threw his arms open involuntarily and said aloud, "Life is beautiful, this is what I call living..." Waiters who had already accepted Nicholas as one of their own were smiling and nodding in agreement. With his arms still open, he turned to the Bosphorus strait and then to Hagia Sophia while focused on Kristen's photo on the screen, and he did not hesitate to proclaim his newly discovered secret, "this is life, I love you Kristen..." However, this time words dropped heavily from his lips and his voice was not as sharp. His mind was boggled.

A man around the dome of Hagia Sophia was moving with something in his hand. Nicholas who had declared his love to the world with arms still extended was watching what was going on without realizing what was taking place. The man, with total disregard of height, was moving fast on top of Hagia Sophia and seemed to be pouring something over the dome. Now arms dropped, Nicholas was glued to the sight. The man stopped every so often and appeared to sprinkle something on the dome from the container in his hand. Who was this man in the middle of the night and how did he climb so high on the temple? Could he be a member of the security personnel? It didn't appear so. Hagia

Sophia was a museum and was lit very well. When looked carefully, one could make out the attire of the man. His attire did not appear very modern. It was as if he was covered head to ankle like a monk. For some strange reason, Nicholas' eyes refocused on Kristen on the computer screen. He sat down slowly. Took a sip from his coffee and gazed warmly at Kristen. Once again he looked at the dome. While he tried to make sense of it all, the man was still sprinkling something. Then he noticed the time on the lower corner of the screen, jumped up in fear and froze. His heart was beating furiously. The man above Hagia Sophia also stood frozen. It appeared he was looking at Nicholas. Then he looked this time at the wrist watch his dad had given him as a gift. Like a miracle, it was exactly 03:27 past midnight...

Now the man was not doing anything. In the middle of the night he had just stood on Hagia Sophia at the edge of the dome and it was as if he was looking at Nicholas. Observing the man with perplexing feelings, Nicholas was searching an answer to his own question: "Is that him? Time is exactly 03:27!"

He had always thought that there was a secret buried in the recurrence of 03:27 in his dreams. But he was never able to discover it. Nicholas' voice trembled, "...the water jug..." The man who just stood waiting on Hagia Sophia with some sort of a container, and just a moment or two ago what he must have been sprinkling from, was surely a sizeable water jug.

Nicholas suddenly left the terrace in haste. Hurried away from the hotel. He was rushing insanely in the void, dark and absolutely silent space just few hours before dawn, not entirely aware what was happening. Then he came to a quick full stop right in front of the famous Sunken Basilica Cistern on the road to Hagia Sophia. Catching his breath for a moment, a line of thought crossed his mind uncontrollably, "Kristen should have seen this deep massive ancient underground water supply cistern with hundreds of high columns still holding it beneath the earth above". In the same moment, he came to realize oddity of what was happening and harshly questioned himself, "Where the hell am I running to?" "Who is this man? What if they are some sort of a weird cult... or an organization?"

He had taken off in a hurry from the hotel without any second thoughts, but now the questions which had been gnawing out his brain since the very beginning once again firmly recaptured his whole being. The agony of conflict with doubt and fear in unison was unbearable indeed.

He felt the need to reassure himself aloud with a fragment of logic conjured in the midst of the night in a several-millennia-old city, thousands of miles away from his native land, and on higher ground than Jerusalem, "No, there are no cults who could captivate dreams and reinject them repeatedly, not even Opus Dei could do this!"

Actually, this was not a new deduction for him. He had been advancing similar logic for self reassurance whenever he encountered difficulties or confusion since the very beginning of his search for the Man Carrying a Water Jug. He was calmer now. Although he was nowhere near of being fully aware or in charge of his senses, he reluctantly continued to walk the recently washed square.

Sultan Ahmet Square or the Hippodrome of Constantinople was absolutely empty, without a single soul around. He was now in front of Hagia Sophia. The iron gates of its garden were locked. He forced them a little. He stepped back a few paces. On the other side of the square stood the Blue Mosque which was just as massive as the Hagia Sophia Basilica. Nicholas headed toward the mosque. Having quickly arrived at the pond on the famous square between the two temples, he stood and wanted to take another look at the

Hagia Sophia dome. He was extremely curious to see if the man was still there. No, he wasn't. Thinking he might have moved around the dome, Nicholas changed his direction. There stood the imperial gates of the Topkapı Palace, now also a museum, from where the immense empire of Turks ruled the vast geographical territories of the middle ages. Modern day soldiers were on guard at the gates. Actually, with the exception of Nicholas, they were the only ones present and he thought, "Sure as hell they must have their eyes on me and wondering what this shadow of a man is doing on the square". Nicholas noticed that the man was not on the other side of Hagia Sophia's dome. Nicholas carefully distanced himself away from the Palace entrance. He walked slowly but with indecisive steps, hands in pockets, as if to create the image of another strange tourist on the side-walk edging the Hagia Sophia garden walls. He stood a little while in front of the gate opened for the tourists during the day visitation hours. He looked at the garden through the iron gate. Just as he decided to give up and return to his hotel, and took a step forward, a voice from the garden uttering the words, "Mr. Nicholas" shook his entire body. The man was beside himself and he was scared stiff. The voice came from the Hagia Sophia garden. His heart was beating furiously in confusion and fear. Once again he tried a careful look at the garden through the gate. He saw someone approaching him. He was stuck still. A man of mid-height, perhaps in his fifties, opened the gate and gently invited him with a very polite hand gesture, "Please sir, do come in, they are waiting for you". Nicholas felt as if he had no choice in the matter and hesitantly took a step in fear. Man in front, he behind him, they began approaching Hagia Sophia. Coming to his senses, Nicholas suddenly stopped. The man was still walking ahead. "Excuse me, who is waiting for me inside? Can you tell me who all you are? What is the meaning of this?"

These were reflex questions flowing out of Nicholas in darkness and fear. Hearing the questions the man also stopped, turned to Nicholas, and as if to suggest disbelief, "Sir... Do you really not know who is waiting for you inside?" The man continued, "... the one who called you for the first time at 03:27 past midnight in your small town Jacksonville house in America..."

These words nailed Nicholas' brain. In one sentence everything was summarized and a special, indisputable message was delivered. The name of his childhood town and the biggest mystery of his life, all in one brief sentence... 03:27.

Man smiling turned back by gently lowering his head. Stopped just for a moment as if to assume his respectful subdued posture and began walking. Nicholas surrendered and followed him with reluctance but no longer in great fear. They arrived after a short walk at the main interior entrance gate. The man stopped. This door Nicholas had seen many times before, but this time it seemed much bigger and mysterious. The legend had it that this was the big door in Noah's ark. When the man began pushing the door open, a noise from the depths of history filled the silent night. When the door was fully open, now stood in front of Nicholas the bright interior which was lit completely. He walked in as he did many times before and there stood another man right under the central chandelier and he was looking at the dome just as Kristen had done. Chandelier was glittering incredibly bright. But, now Nicholas' eyes were locked on another point, the object held by the man standing in the center of the temple beneath the dome, the water jug... There it was, now his dream was certainly a reality. Nicholas' throat was as dry as desert soil. The man who led him in from the garden stepped aside and politely pointed at the center and gently ushered him saying, "Please, Mr. Nicholas". Nicholas moved forward slowly with a strong feeling of reverence and respect mixed with fear. Then a sudden noise from behind startled him. Quickly glimpsing back, he noticed that the door was shut again and the man who had brought him in was gone. He refocused his attention to the host who invited him and slowly continued stepping forward towards the Man Carrying a Water Jug at the center of the temple.

Nicholas was trembling uncontrollably. He approached until a respectful distance was left between them. He was a man of mid-height, perhaps in his late seventies or early eighties, silver white hair, eye-brows and a moustache. He had no beard. He had on him what appeared to be a modest Dervish's ankle length crudely woven, simple cardigan suggesting total disregard of the material world. The old man's gaze was piercing as if he was reading Nicholas' soul. On his right hand, he was holding a mid-size earthen water jug with a reversed earthen cup acting as a lid. Nicholas had seen this detail in his dreams many times before. For sure his dream was now a reality.

"Welcome," he said with a gentle but sharp voice although somewhat constrained. The tone of his voice was very pleasant and effective.

Nicholas didn't know what he could or should say. He was caught in the twilight of reality and mystery with countless questions storming inside his confused and turbulent mind. The old man who stood firm like embodiment of wisdom and looked piercingly at Nicholas' eyes spoke with words equally effective, "I know you are confused, I know you have numerous questions for which you are seeking answers, but I suggest you refrain from asking questions, otherwise the journey will end…"

Nicholas in the vortex of fear was unable to resist the urge to at least direct one little question as if begging a favor, "Leonardo Da Vinci also warned in his book not to ask questions, not to object but I really want to ask a very simple question…"

The wise man smiled gently and said, "He was asking too many questions and vehemently objected to what I had told him about women. Finally he saw the reality, but it was too late. Of course, I will answer a few of your questions…"

Drawn in with immense relief, Nicholas as if wanting to resolve the whole mystery with one stroke, immediately posed his question, "All these, my continuously repeating dream, what is the meaning of it? Please, who are you? To where is the journey?"

Still smiling, the old man replied, "very justified questions" and continued "the reason for all of this is the imagination you constructed with your pure innocent heart free of sin, and with your mind while you were a just a little child. You prayed to the Creator with your imagination and he rewarded you with his love, bicycles, money, trips to here and there... Your dream was to have your prayers accepted."

Nicholas couldn't help but smile with a gentle sorrow in his heart at these words. These were the sweet memories of his childhood. After a brief silence the Man Carrying a Water Jug said, "Your dream was the acceptance of all your prayers. Here it is, it has been granted. Now I will show you the secret of the acceptance of your prayers".

The old man slowly turned and stepped forward from the center of Hagia Sophia, also gesturing at Nicholas to follow him. Nicholas paced after him slowly in total submission. The old man's pleasant voice began echoing softly in the temple as he continued to speak, "What we call journey is the time we will spend together and places we will see. As for who I am, you already know this well, you have been searching for me for many years. I am the Man Carrying a Water Jug..."

Nicholas was still as confused as ever. He tried not to show it, but he was still fearful. The Man Carrying a Water Jug mentioned in the Bible lived at the time of Jesus, how could he be alive today? His mind didn't comprehend it. What was this, it couldn't be a game for sure. It couldn't be, no one could have anyone see the same dream years on end. Just as he attempted to further press the point and just as the words, "yes, but how could this be?" uncontrollably dropped out of his lips, the old man turned quickly gesturing to him to remain silent. It was now clear that he didn't want any further trivial questions. Having already turned toward Nicholas just at arm's length, he affectionately touched the young man and said, "I understand you, you have many questions on your mind. But, you must find the answers not with questions but through the journey". His hands were soft as cotton.

When Nicholas heard the words, "You have been captured by a mighty feeling. It is visible in your eyes", he was even more perplexed and looked as if he was totally lost. When he continued, "You have been captivated by that magnificent feeling. Your eyes are speaking of love and admitting that you have fallen in love", Nicholas couldn't hold back and while thinking of Kristen again he retorted innocently, "Really, is it visible in my eyes?"

Old man smiling, "Of course, eyes never lie and they converse best". They had already arrived at the front section of the temple. The wise man softly touched the walls and together they walked slowly towards the left side of the building. Following a short silence, the wise man's sweet voice began echoing softly again, "*I love you*. This is a very serious statement, a heavy declaration. Shouldn't be said easily to everyone. Sometimes it is necessary to wait many years for those three simple words... It burns the tongue, the lips, the body, tears you apart... It is for the brave hearts... Be careful, those words must be said to one person in a lifetime even if it costs a life. And when possible, these incredible words should not come into contact with air, otherwise they lose their magic. It should only be said from eye to eye and from heart to heart so long as you live..."

When these words were unified with the pleasant voice of this man from the world of dreams, Nicholas' mind, already in the vortex of excitement and fear, was further numbed. Helplessly he responded at once as if to seek forgiveness, "I am in love, but I do not know love. I don't know if what I had lived before was love or not?" and quickly added, "I am very sorry, I didn't mean to interrupt. Your words affected me greatly".

The old man smiled affectionately and said in his magical voice:

"If your fluttering heart rise to sweet heavens or fall deep in a dark void when you recall her...

If like a trepidatious butterfly with life measured in hours, day long you settle on that sorrow or this joy due to love with no apparent reason...

If the furious blades of time which spin devouringly are nailed motionless in your love's absence like a scorpion's treason...

If shyness rushes your face, your soul transcends your being, if a word of your love reduces you to sulking or give you a mischievous smile anywhere...

And if your love stands with you wherever you may be, look back at you from everywhere, laugh or cry with you...

If the best place on Earth is where your love is, if the best aroma is the sweet smell of shared sweat, and if the most horrendous feeling is the sorrow in your love's eyes...

If life is beautiful or suffers addiction without it...

If apples, roof tiles, the sky, the earth are rose pink and her face is also rose pink...

If winter is spring, summer is spring, autumn is spring...

If she is what every poem depicts, if she is each hero, if every novel is describing her, if each song tells about her...

If a momentary separation feels like a lifetime, and at the very second of departure if longing pulls your hair at the roots and hurts your brain...

If you lose, regain and lose your appetite again all the time...

If you are living with your hand on the phone, always dialing and if you dream of the same person every time the door rings...

If you are startled with every phone ring, if the best attire on the window suits only her, if you are sighing at your heart when you hear someone else talk and wish it was her telling you...

If not for a moment her aroma in your nose, image on your eyes, voice in your ears and touch of her skin in your mind abandon your thoughts...

If longing for your love fries your heart and intoxicates your brain...

If at the beginning you hide her but later wish that everyone knew...

If the nights are without a soul, sparkless and streets are orphaned...

If no sacrifice is too great, no road too long, and nothing worth more...

Then, you are in the arms of that most sacred feeling"

Having finished his words, the old man turned back slowly. Nicholas was mesmerized. He felt Kristen nearby at each word said. Her face, her voice, her presence...

The wise old man touched Nicholas in a fatherly manner. "You are in love with Kristen... Eyes do not lie" and continued walking slowly. They arrived at the stone paved spiral climb in the temple. Nicholas was startled and he was instantly confronted with a silent question since he had not revealed any name to the old man, "In love with Kristen? How did he know about Kristen?" Yet he did not have the courage to pose the question.

Mysterious man was walking slowly up the spiral ramp towards the second floor of the temple and Nicholas was following respectfully and hesitantly right behind him in mixed feelings. Even in this strange situation Kristen was ever present on his mind. Her eyes, voice and her sweet smile...

For what appeared to be a long time, this walk continued in silence. At the entrance of the second floor, the man suddenly came to halt and said, "You know Nicholas, women are the least understood creatures in this world".

Nicholas did not know how to respond. Let alone what to say, his mind was totally blank. Man stepped forward again slowly. They were now on the second floor. Although the temple was lit in the midst of the night, below it looked rather gloomy. Deep prevailing silence was disrupted with the coarse voice of the man, "Let me tell you the secret of women. It'll be short and I'll mention only a few. Later I'll tell you all of it in detail. Thus you will understand the secret of Leonardo's reason for drawing Mona Lisa mentioned in the book and also give the respect and love deserved by Kristen". They were leaning on the marble parapet on the second wall and looking below. Nicholas was still struggling in the vortex of his bedevilment. He was also anxious to hear what was about to be said on women.

It seemed as if sounds were echoing more here. The man's voice in the night had become a resonance penetrating one's soul, "Never disregard this: The only guilt of Eve is obedience to a man. It was Adam who succumbed to the devil appearing as a snake. Not Eve... If you fail to understand this, then you will never appreciate the beauty and magnificence of women. This clearly explains a hidden truth to those who are able to see and comprehend. It seems you fail to grasp it..."

It was true, Nicholas failed to grasp it fully and was looking with inquisitive eyes. This was the opposite of what he knew and read. Leonardo Da Vinci had also said something like "this is against my religious doctrine".

The old man, gently smiling, continued his explanation:

"When story of the forbidden fruit, the apple, was being told, intentionally or unintentionally, wrong information was mixed in it. At the place and time where Jesus lived women were seen as objects of sex, never respected, humiliated and were bought and sold. Jesus wanted to change this situation. Many ordinary ignorant men did not like what Jesus was saying about women. Rich and powerful men also did not approve of it. The status which had befallen women well suited this mob. These evil men extended their accusations even to Mary Magdalene. Their aim was to belittle women again through Magdalena. But, the truth was very different. The reality was that it had been a wonderful love.

Forbidden apple was actually eaten by Adam. The devil had tricked Adam through Eve. The devil had no problems with Eve. He was competing with Adam for superiority.

Adam was madly in love with Eve... So much so that nothing else mattered. Only Eve...

The devil tricked Adam with the promise that he would become immortal and live with Eve forever if he should eat the fruit "forbidden by God". Upon eating the forbidden apple, Adam's genitalia awakened. He immediately covered himself with tree leaves. He spoke of it to Eve. Neither Adam, nor Eve wanted to be apart, they were both madly in love... Eve was devoted to Adam. Eve knowingly ate the forbidden fruit simply because

Adam wanted it, not because of the devil. She just did not want to be different than her lover. She braved the consequences of her action simply because of her love. She was willing to face the punishment promised by God. She was not tricked by nor did she believe in the devil.

There are no words which could describe such a sacrifice and courage. Jesus had thus spoken of this event to his nearest friends."

Nicholas was shocked. What he heard was totally contrary to his knowledge of religion and he couldn't hold back, "But the Bible doesn't say so." These words abruptly came out as pure and sincere thoughts of a young faithful man who believed in the Bible.

The old man was amused, "Do you not see, you were surprised at Leonardo for objecting to such a man for what had been said about women. You too are objecting…"

Nicholas lowered his head in embarrassment. Indeed, he had found Leonardo's objection surprising and did not understand his mistake, but he had only just thought of it. Nicholas knew certainly that he had not mentioned this to anyone. Not even to Michael...

The wise old man took a deep breath. "Alas! You only read. Never think. Times have changed and now you have the luxury of reaching any information with a single pressing of a button. But you do not seriously question the details and ponder. The Bible you hold in your hands was written between 40-80AD by the first hand witnesses. They are similar. It concerns Jesus' life and teachings. Mark is the shortest part. Mark had not been near Jesus. He was a student of Peter. He describes vividly Peter's sermons and Jesus' teachings. Mark was written in 50-55AD. You could see from the Latin words that it was written in Rome. Matthew is one of the 12 disciples. He is also known as Levi. He wrote the Bible in Aramaic in 45 AD for the education and evangelization of Jews, later it was translated into Greek around 50-55 AD for wider use.

Matthew was a pious and educated man, a tax collector devoted to the Old Testament. Luke was a physician and historian. He was the only non-Jew. He was from Antioch and a student of Paul. He is the author of the extension. It was written around 61-62 AD. Johannes is one of the 12 disciples. He wrote in Greek at Ephesus around 69 AD. He wrote the best loved section by the devoted faithful. He speaks of seven miracles witnessed by many. Until old age, he had followed Jesus and written what he had seen."

Now the old man had stopped and a deep silence took over the temple. Just as Nicholas failed to think, "Why did he explain all of this? Was a history lesson necessary?" The man spoke again:

"Matthew, Mark, Luke and Johannes were believers. Some had the honor of living with Jesus. They were very valuable persons. But they were also mortals. They were writing Jesus' teachings and what they had witnessed. But they also included their own commentaries. In time, new words kept being added to the books for ease of understanding. But there was something which had gone unnoticed. Jesus occasionally spoke in ciphers. These unnoticed ciphers were further complicated with these commentaries and vital information given by Jesus reached today's people in contrary meanings. Although the apple was eaten first by Adam, those who failed to understand the deep love accused Eve. Jesus had given a deep secret..."

Nicholas was awed and impatiently listening. After a brief silence the old man continued:

"Indeed, Jesus had given his disciples secretive information. Speaking of it openly would have distanced people from him at a time when women were bought and sold like worthless objects. But he also wanted to show the correct path to the people and invite them to God. For this reason he used cipher and spoke of women thus, 'Woman was created by God from the rib of Adam'. They failed to understand this incredible secret. It was thought that this placed woman in a secondary and a lower position as if she was meant to be a slave of man. This interpretation spread wildly. It still is seen as such. Jesus was screaming a truth to those who could grasp its essence and understand, 'Behold mankind, Adam was created from earth but the woman was not. She was created from another substance..."

Nicholas was speechless. Even the Pope had spoken recently of the potential of misinterpretations in the Bible. This suggested secrets in the Bible. It seemed Jesus had ciphered some parts of the new religion only for those who could really grasp it when it was too contrary to the convictions of people to avoid distancing them."

The old man began walking to the section on the right of temple from where they were looking below. The only sound was that of Nicholas' shoes on the marble floor. When they reached the section with fresco a little ahead, the man's pleasant voice filled the temple again:

"God and his messengers first convert the message into a material form. They describe it in accordance with people's comprehension capacity and their lives. When he said Adam was created from earth, He meant that all molecular ingredients were present in the soil. This was what Jesus meant. It was not a sculpture from mud. When he spoke of Eve being created from a rib, what he really meant was women were not created from soil and that they had a different substance, that they were of a completely different creation. Pointing at Adam's rib what he really was saying that 'Faithful men, know that women were created specially. They are different. You can be a whole only with your woman. She is a part of you. You will be incomplete without them just as you will be incomplete in the absence of a bone in your body', but they interpreted this incorrectly, failed to understand specialty of women. They still do not understand magnificence of women."

Nicholas was extremely excited with what he had heard and erupted, "In other words, there is no such thing as woman being created from a rib. Women were created from an entirely different substance. Jesus spoke of it as such in order to cipher it. He meant men would be incomplete without women. He ciphered it that way because of the prevailing circumstances and offered it to those who could understand it." As Nicholas was uttering these words, they arrived in front of the fresco of Jesus.

The old man looked at Nicholas affectionately and said, "Exactly. You understood it correctly."

Nicholas, wanting to resolve all the questions on his mind, was looking at the man standing with respect in front of the fresco of Jesus. Who was this man? Could he be the Man Carrying a Water Jug mentioned in the Bible? It couldn't be, that was not possible. Nobody could be alive that long. Then, who was he? What about the incredible information he had just revealed? Wrestling with the questions on his mind, Nicholas did not know how to respond to the question posed by the old man turning towards him, "One feels a great pleasure when he watches a woman's body...Why?"

Nicholas lowered his eyes surprised and a little embarrassed. He stuttered a little and was only able to say respectfully, "I do not know".

"Yes, one feels a great pleasure watching a female body. Who are you watching? This is a secret... how could you know...you have just been informed about this being a cipher...", and the old man bent slightly in reverence and departed. Nicholas repeated the same gesture and walked after him.

Man advancing in small and slow steps interrupted Nicholas' mixed thoughts with another abrupt question:

"Nicholas, do you know what *aendahm* means?"

Nicholas had never heard of this unusual word before. Old man obviously aware that no answer would be forthcoming continued, "There is an invisible amazing order in the body of a woman, there is a divine harmony. There is an incredible form and glory. This is called *aendahm*. Aendahm is the whole. Without defect... Magical... God created woman with this most beautiful aendahm. This is the reason why all women are very beautiful.

Spiritual aendahm, and its beauty, surfaces in the hair of women... Hair is the reflection of a woman's inner beauty. One can see a woman's inner beauty in her hair... Spiritual aendahm of a woman is most formidable. God's most beautiful creation is women. For God, there are no unattractive women. All women are beautiful. **But if they only knew how to use water.. .pure water... they could preserve their aendahm**".

When Nicholas heard the word "water", he immediately recalled its large inscriptions in each page of Leonardo's 'Book of Secrets'. He also thought of the section in it from the Bible about 'water'. He wondered about the secret of the 'water' in the old man's speech. Just as they headed slowly down the spiral ramp, the wise man was still talking:

"Aendahm... This word has been created for women only. If women had been created from a male rib, they would have exhibited male-like features but none do... You understand don't you, their organs are also different... very different", and slowly turned looking at Nicholas. His stare was very sharp. As they were reaching the floor of temple, the old man continued:

"Why do women have naturally beautiful hair?"

With the silence disrupting sermon, Nicholas hesitated to answer. He intuitively knew that it really did not matter. He did not have an answer. Obviously the old man was also of the same opinion. He continued on:

"A woman with long hair has a unique beauty. They enjoy this. Why? Some women in India and Spain never cut their hair. These women have honor and they are dangerous...Why?"

Nicholas had no answer to give. The old man was not in the mood to wait for one. Just as they stepped on the temple floor, after a momentary pause, he continued:

"Women of India have a dangerous devotion. You must fear an Indian woman in love. She is capable of anything. Spanish woman knows to die for her love and to kill for denial. This is because they do not cut their hair. Hair is the reflection of inner beauty not externalized."

They were now on the main floor. Nicholas just did not know how to respond to what he had heard. He was stupidified by these mysterious words while he had so many unanswered questions and while the secrets of Leonardo's book were still intact. He wanted to pursue the thought by saying, "OK, what is the secret of women's hair?" but he was forewarned by Leonardo, "do not ask too many questions, or the journey will end." Nicholas had the sense that Leonardo was unhappy with early termination of his journey. He was also forewarned by the old man's instruction: "Do not ask questions. Solve them yourself during the journey." Just as he was wrestling with the thought "fine, how the hell am I going to solve the secret of women's hair", he was jerked with the man's voice:

"Woman. Home. Family. These are the greatest blessings given to men by God. Holiest temple on earth is family and home. Woman is the foundation of family and nation, ornament and wealth of home. Sincere and respectful love for women is the holiest worship. That's because a woman is a man's most precious richness and the greatest blessing of God. Everything beautifies a woman, Nicholas. Earrings, accessories, shoes, eye makeup, hair styles... all of these suit women. But what suits a man most is the woman next to him. There is nothing else that befits a man more than a woman. A woman is endowed with sense of respectability, love, affection and support. They are born with sense of motherhood. Order and harmony are part of their creation. Men are also endowed with feelings of protection, supplying the needs of family, preserving family honor and continuity. Family happiness is a concept unique to humans. If a man loves a woman and adorns her like a crown over his head, then the woman loves him back. Loving is more difficult than causing conflict. Cabinet drawers are not the places for family memories.

The man continued talking while they were walking slowly at the ground level.

"God created women with beautiful aendahm. Greatest blessing for man's worship to be near God is his woman. Man's most precious wealth is his woman. Man must make her happy. Loving a woman is a great worship. God says, 'he who loves his woman also loves me'. There is deep meaning in this. While you love them, you might not know that you have also loved God. If a woman is pleased with you, then God is also pleased with you. These were the words of Jesus."

Nicholas had neither heard these words from someone else nor did he see any such words in all the books he had read. He was being intoxicated when these wise words unified in his mind with the effective voice of the old man, and feelings mobilized all of his emotions. "Close your eyes when you kiss a woman. This is God's word. Why should eyes be closed? Learn the great reason..."

Nicholas know this well, "...Loving and being loved is the most important worship."

Slowly they had arrived at the front of the Basilica. This was the section where nice additions had been made centuries ago by the great grandfathers of present day Turks. The man halted right in front of this section which was just a short flight above the ground level. There was a deep silence. Gently and slowly he sat on the riser just ahead of him. Nicholas was facing him in great respect and impatient to hear the remainder. The man's gaze floated at the temple dome for an extended period. Finally lowered his eyes and began speaking as he fixed his stare on Nicholas' eyes:

"Marriage is a worship of wedlock commanded by God. Woman is a man's means of worship for reaching God. Man loves his woman, gives children and happiness to her in the nest. These are the types of worship. Union of couples in spirit and body with desires and feelings is also worship. Body is the shrine of spirit. Woman is the gate of this shrine. Comprehension of this is most difficult for many. Loving begins with unadulterated true love. This is unification of two separate persons. First, the spirits unite. Then the bodies… This is the joy of reaching absolute being. This is the absolute freedom indescribable with words. This is only possible with true love for one woman. It is the frontier of happiness nearing God. Unification of both sides with mutual love and desire is worship. Than the moment of relief is like embracing God."

"Embracing God?" Nicholas suddenly questioned. His mind and logic caused him respond in a moment failing to grasp what was said. He recoiled and wanting to appear as if he was not posing a question he added quickly, "Excuse me, I had never heard such beautiful words concerning especially sexuality. I didn't mean to suggest a question, it was a momentary surprise…"

Smiling affectionately, the old man simply said, "you haven't heard a word, did you?" and continued to elaborate, "... humans shall live that very moment's joy thousand fold in paradise. God made this pleasure an example of what awaits believers in paradise. Body cannot survive intensity of this pleasure for long, this is why it lasts only for a very short while. If you read the Bible well you will see that Jesus speaks of this indirectly. "

Who was this man? Nicholas hadn't heard such words anywhere else. Each word revealed a new mystery.

The wise man stood abruptly. They had been walking at a fairly slow pace since their meeting, but now he was walking much faster. Nicholas matched his speed and followed him closely. They stopped in front of a supporting column. Smiling, the old man caressed the column gently. This was the same column with people in line that Nicholas had seen upon his first visit to the temple. This was the place where people made wishes by rotating their hands anti-clockwise in the column's crevice. He, too, had made a wish. This was the column known as the "perspiring pillar". Old man turned around the pillar once with his right hand rubbing the column and proceeded forward. Nicholas was right behind and observing him. He kept wondering "Now what happened at the Perspiring Pillar? Why did he stop there? Why did he turn around it?"

He did have many questions, but he was unable to ask. They stepped outside from the large gate. As the old man sped up, sounds were heard from the earthen jug he had been holding on his side all this time. It was the sound of water splashing within the jug. Nicholas was eagerly awaiting to hear new things, but the only sounds which disrupted the silence was his own footsteps and the sound of water arising from the jug.

They were now in the temple garden. They slowly paced to the pool surrounded with fountains. This pool was covered with a dome of its own but was held with narrower columns allowing access to the pool. The man sat on a low stool located in front of a fountain. Nicholas was standing in semi-darkness and watching him attentively. Man first washed his hands with utmost care as if he was in a trance. Sprinkled water to his face for a long period. Gently wetted his silvery white hair by slowly passing his fingers through. Washed his hands again. Leaned to his side and took the water jug. Slowly removed the cup which was being used as the tap of earthen jug, filled it with water from the jug and began drinking. He was taking big gulps and he breathed deeply for extended periods. It was as if a master gourmet was tasting the most delicious food on earth and enjoying every little morsel exceedingly. The old man was closing his eyes as he took large sips and reopened them after swallowing. Nicholas couldn't help thinking in a moment's disregard and disrespect "he is only drinking water but acts as if he is enjoying beefsteak with sauce."

The old man drank the water in the cup slowly, and as usual, placed the cup upside down on the jug and continued:

"Nicholas, if you look at man's history and consider even the most barbarous tribes or the most civilized, the most advanced countries or the least developed, largest empires or the smallest kingdoms, you will see that they conform to an ancient principle. Among the wars of these you will never see women at the line of fire. They are not allowed to war. Of course, women were behind the lines and contributed immensely but they were not allowed at the front lines. This was the result of knowledge inherited from ancient times. This was an ancient rule, a commandment of God and a prohibition subject to his fury and punishment. In time its reason was forgotten, but the rule survived. It was forgotten that this had been God's commandment and eventually it was said "women are weak and fragile. We will not allow them to fight in the front lines". But the reality was different, there used to be a divine rule which said, "For whatever reason, those who kill women shall never be forgiven...This was a certain warning from God. Jesus had also spoke of this to those around him. This is an important fact for you to realize how special creation women are. God never forgives someone who kills a woman, especially a girl child. Repentance or penitence is never possible for this evil and sin. This is God's word..."

Nicholas having heard this incredible information for the first time interrupted in amazement, "unbelievable, I've always assumed women's exclusion from wars was due to their weak constitution."

There was a sharp moment of extended silence. The old man sorrowfully smiled a little: "regretfully, in order to disguise women's special status in God's eyes, they concocted lies claiming women's weakness, delicateness and lack of physical prowess. God's severe warning was erased from minds of men."

Appearing tired of his many years, the wise man stood up slowly. Hesitantly stepped ahead in the shadowy night garden. Nicholas followed right behind with Kristen on one corner of his mind, intensity of the words he had just heard on the other, but with a deep sense of shame for attributing 'beefsteak with sauce' to the Old Man's thirst which appeared to be old age. What if the man had sensed his offence?

It didn't appear so as the old man continued: "God never forgives those who kill women, especially girl children, never... never... never... This is God's Words..." He did repeat thrice the firm commandment as if to suggest much evil had occurred over time and guilt had flooded the Earth. Nicholas couldn't precisely and fully understand the Old Man's reasoning behind repeating the words thrice, but the young New Yorker was now in enough command of his senses to refrain from adding a comment or question. It was definitely not a moment for Nicholas to push his luck, not even in genuine innocence. Words kept flowing from semi-lit shadowy darkness of the Hagia Sophia night. The temple now appeared to stand proud sky high, a solid witness of times long gone and hearing the old man profess mysteries long forgotten:

"Men must treat women well. Never torment women. Those who oppress women or act cruelly, those who tyrannize women, those who persecute women, suppress, limit or belittle shall have no fair end...devoid of any forgiveness... Their lives shall be an inferno distant from any peace of heart or soul.. Certainly they shall be the ones reduced to nothing at the end of their lives... Woman is to be loved, that's all...Loving a woman is a great worship of real men. Women are ornaments from God's Heaven. Keep them happy, hold them in respect as equals and love them generously. They are beautiful and this beauty must be acknowledged as God's miracle. They have been granted aendahm by the Creator, they have been formed with aendahm in God's delicate proportions. These were the words of Jesus..."

Stopped abruptly, turned to Nicholas, while remaining silent stared piercingly in darkness at his eyes clearly measuring the expanse of Nicholas' soul, than as if satisfied, the words flowed again one by one, this time intermittently as if they were being drawn out of immense depths:

"Do not force yourselves on women...Not unless she desires...Never invade women... Aggression against women is a great sin... There is no penitence and forgiveness for this... No one is capable of burying and hiding their sins beneath the earth...."

Appearing to have finished his words, the Old Man followed the garden wall with slow steps. Then added unexpectedly, "these too were God's words and this was what Jesus said…" Then again he repeated the same thrice. It was as if he wanted Nicholas to memorize them…

"Do not force yourselves on women… Not unless she desires… Never invade women… Aggression against women is a great sin… There is no penitence and forgiveness for this… No one is capable of burying and hiding their sins beneath the earth.…"

Nicholas was speechless. He thought, "then, this thing called equality of men and women must also be a concoction. This may have also been said to camouflage women's special place in God's eyes… Making men equal to women… to stain women… perhaps to erase women's special place…"

Then suddenly he recalled Leonardo's words in the "Book of Secrets" where he was saying "…I was so affected and influenced with what was said that night, I would have fallen in love with the first woman I see on the street and kiss her feet…" Now, Nicholas did not find these words of Leonardo strange or odd.

Nicholas was now somewhat comforted and kept thinking with a pleasing muse which had suddenly settled on his slight smile caused by this privileged encounter, "He told me of secrets about women, promised he will speak of it more… I, too, am ready to fall in love this very moment with the first woman I see if it weren't for Kristen…" Nicholas was unable to erase from his face the pleasure of contentment.

As they walked together, now they were on the left side section of Hagia Sophia garden. The Old Man guided himself with by gently touching the wall. Right behind, Nicholas mimicked him exactly as if wanting to capture any special powers which might exist. On the immediate left the ancient wall of Topkapı Palace rose high. It was nearing dawn. The Old Man stood in front of the small gate little ahead. He had a key in his hand which Nicholas hadn't noticed earlier. Opened the gate. Gestured at Nicholas to follow as he stepped through. After a short walk in a narrow stone-built corridor they slowly climbed the stone stairs, the Old Man still leading. The door facing them was unlocked by him, and he stepped in a small, cavernous room followed by Nicholas. The walls were covered by volumes of old books. The interior had a unique odor, a mystical aroma of history as if it were. The old Man approached an old table in the center of the room. Slowly opened a drawer. With great care, he began pulling out an object which Nicholas couldn't see. Then the Old Man slowly and gently placed on the table an object wrapped in bright yellow cloth. When the Old Man opened the wrapping Nicholas relived a moment as if he saw again the "Book of Secrets" he had left in his hotel room. Now much nearer to observe the book on the table, he realized that it was identical to the one he had recovered at the Mount Olive. The only difference was that this one had cleaner cloth covering. The writings, its size, its ornamentation, everything was identical. For a moment he was terrified, he thought aloud once again and uttered, "how did this book locked in the hotel case arrive here?"

The Old Man smiled mysteriously, "Be calm and patient. This is not that book. That one belonged to Leonardo... This one shall be yours..."

Nicholas failed to grasp what was said. It could have been easily seen on his shocked facial expression. Already he was far removed from this world after all that he had heard about women. Old Man took out from the drawer what appeared to be a pen. Nicholas whispered cautiously and gently: "beautiful". Indeed, the pen was very different and beautiful. It was much thicker than those

Nicholas was familiar with. It appeared to have been made of a material like glass. It had bright yellow decorative insignia etched on it. It contained a soft moving viscous dark blue liquid mixed with what appeared to be gilding powder.

The Old Man held the pen close to Nicholas' eyes holding it from the center with two aged fingers. Turned it clockwise once and immediately added, "You see? While writing this book, when one page finishes and before you begin a new page you must not forget to hold this pen from its exact center and turn it once clockwise..." Nicholas did not hesitate to immediately acknowledge this ciphered instruction which also appeared as a command which needed to be kept confidential. But, Nicholas was impatiently waiting for further instructions on what needed to be written in this ancient book.

The Old Man touched reassuringly at Nicholas' shoulder and as if he had read Nicholas' mind and soul he said, "You will write in this book what you learn from me during our journey together and only my words. You will only write in this book when the moon is in full, when nights are free of clouds and at times when the pen receives clear direct moon light. There shall be no other light around, only the moon light..." Nicholas could not think of another time in his life when he was so absorbed in such bewildering and incredible feelings.

The Old Man stepped a little ahead and slowly sat at the simple chair. He now looked as an aging master instructing a young and talented apprentice. Indicated to Nicholas with a soft and simple gesture that the apprentice may now take the book and the pen from the table. Nicholas took the book and pen with utmost care and in great reverence, his deep and matured respect for his Guide was clearly evident. He held the book in his left hand near his chest like an eager ancient monastery pupil, and the pen with delicate care in his right hand.

Then Nicholas received further instructions, "Now go. Spend a nice and happy day with Kristen and her flighty friend. In the evening see her off safely and with gentle care to your homeland, to America. Rest well and be here exactly at 03:27 past midnight."

Even though Nicholas had million questions, this time he knew to keep his mouth shut and with great obedience he replied respectfully like a soldier, "Yes, Sir. I shall definitely be here."

Just as he was about to leave, the coarse but beautiful voice of the Old Man resonated in the cavernous stone walled room possibly older than 15 centuries.

"Nicholas, a woman is the only angel of a man. Do not seek winged angels, fairies and genies here and there... Just look at women, look at Kristen!"

Just before noon he met Kristen and Amber at the Hippodrome of Constantinople adjacent to Hagia Sophia. Nicholas was beside himself and near speechless when confronted with friendly Kristen whose eyes were smiling sincerely.

Amber spoke bluntly as usual and giggling she said, "looks like we have a hangover from last night, eyes so swollen and everything".

Nicholas tried to explain, ".... a little sleepless night, that's why!"

Not only lack of sleep was visible in his eyes, but he also felt the night's exhaustion all over his body. His mind was tired of struggling with questions of mangled and endless mysteries. He was unable to resolve how the Man Carrying a Water Jug mentioned in the Bible could be existing in this era. Just a few hours ago, he had returned from Hagia Sophia to his hotel trembling before dawn. Although his mind was mixed up with a fearful anxiety, he examined for a fairly long time in his room that mystical, equally beautiful pen. Blue liquid in the pen flowed very gently as the pen moved and a colorful racketing jamboree was displayed among the yellow gild ornamentation on its glass reservoir. And strangely this display distanced one from thinking, almost like being absorbed, pulled in against one's will.

After having locked the book and pen given by the man in the hotel-room safe, he had his breakfast enjoying the full view of city's scenic panorama on the upper floor, prepared and arrived here to meet Kristen and Amber.

A mischievous smile landed on Amber's face after she blurted, "Don't worry, you aren't the only one who couldn't sleep". Thinking it would be impolite, he couldn't inquire by asking "Who couldn't sleep?" As if wanting to change his tired appearance, he reverenced the ladies with an inviting smile and said "Alright then ladies, are you ready for a fantastic day? An excursion with the world's best guide –I mean me- is about to begin".

Their excursion which began at this historical square continued including the Topkapı Palace from which the Ottoman Empire once administered a large territory extending from Africa to Egypt, from Iraq to Vienna; mysterious Sunken Cistern of Byzantium, Galata Tower of the Genovese, Egyptian Bazaar in which an endless variety of delicious spices are sold, the imperial Yıldız Palace, the off-shore Maiden's Tower resembling a tiny castle which had witnessed a legendary love affair, locales of entertainment and historical sites, and the famous Taksim. It was as if time just flew by with Kristen. Laughter and chit-chat, photographs one after another.... A beautiful day spent by talking all day long, humor and jokes, endless compliments, childhood stories told at moments invariably beginning with the line, "… in our town when I was little…", and conversations held with magical connection of eyes. They had an opportunity to understand each other better.

The dinner they had on a beautiful ship in the sight of incredible Bosphorus scenery was the grand finale of this pleasant excursion. As the ship glided on the waters of Bosphorus, the waterfront mansions and palaces of the empire added a unique ambiance to this mystical city.

During dinner Amber was talking about the last book she read. It was evident that she was very affected by that book. When Amber put it plainly as "I am gonna do just like Elizabeth Gilbert. Go around and write a book: Eat, Drink, Pray and F... The Rest"; Kristen couldn't withhold herself and a storm of laughter erupted among all three.

"A book title one would expect from you" spurted Kristen chuckling in laughter. Nicholas, too, was sincere part of it all but he was more preoccupied with joyous Kristen who in his mind had become a different, a more angelic person:

> "Oh, love! How I adore each graceful iota of thee...
> Fear my own gaze whilst thinking it might harm thee...
> If only I could lay beneath your feet the universe entirely...
> May evil eye be far and God's blessings be upon you...
> Oh angel descendent from heaven, how beautiful art thou."

If only Kristen could also hear this inner voice rising in him. He really wanted very much to say, "Kristen, I love you, I'm in love with you".

Nicholas' mind began trickstering again and numbed, disabling him from hearing what Kristen was saying. It was as if a symphonic orchestra was playing a magnificent love melody within his ears, and he desired to declare his love to Kristen, the Bosphorus and everyone aboard the ship just as he had done to the whole city that night at the top floor of his hotel.

"Did you read?" asked Amber. With this voice he jerked and came to his senses. As if to confirm he was forced to say "Read what?"

Amber continued laughing, "…night's sleep deprivation is continuing in a flight. Where is our gentleman?"

Nicholas couldn't say anything.

Kristen jumped in as if wanting to save Nicholas from a tight spot, "… talking about the book: Eat Pray Love…"

Nicholas retorted "Yes, I've read it. Nice book".

Kristen was looking at the unequaled scenery of the Bosphorus when she suddenly said, "I prefer Da Vinci's Code".

Amber replied without hesitation, "Yeah… It's incredible".

Kristen continued saying, "Leonardo Da Vinci is a person filled with mysteries and secrets, and he appears to have reflected these to his works".

Amber reaffirmed, "Yes sweetheart, I agree… Fantastic…"

Now that topic was Leonardo, Nicholas was careful not to miss a word said. Kristen carried on, "You know, something really got me curious, when you enlarge and examine Mona Lisa painting, you can actually see over her shoulder at a distance behind an old arched stone bridge. I've been thinking ever since what that seemingly irrelevant bridge might be trying to say."

Amber giggled mischievously saying, "don't you think he has other things do, why would he bother with an arched bridge? What could he possibly express with a 'bridge'?" Then, pointing at Kristen she said, "our art historian professor here, very interested in mysterious things…"

"You are very quick in making fun, aren't you?" Kristen shot back a little irritated and slightly embarrassed in front of Nicholas.

Amber tried to soothe her saying, "Don't be pissed girl, sweetheart it's a joke, a joke..." and held Kristen's hand with a loving gesture. Nicholas aware of touchy situation cut in right away, "I think Leonardo is pointing at the location where he sketched Mona Lisa. I bet the bridge was in his view while he was drawing".

While Amber laughed out "another mystery tracker", Kristen said "I agree, most likely it points at a location, but I feel there must also be something else. A genius like Da Vinci won't draw a bridge just to point at a location..."

Nicholas excited with the secrets he came upon during the past weeks was eager to reveal carefully, "I heard from some people that Leonardo drew that painting by looking at a woman's figurine depicted in a mosaic. Contrary to what most believe, it is not the painting of a living woman... Zeugma is a town from antiquity here in Turkey. During the excavations they have uncovered magnificent mosaic paintings. They are exhibited in the museum. I was there and saw them. Incredible paintings. You know? That mosaic which Leonardo was inspired to draw Mona Lisa is also at the museum".

Strangely, Amber was first to reply in disbelief, "Come on... You are bullshitting".

At the same moment Kristen's eyes sparked, "Are you sure? I'm serious, if this is true the whole world will go on rampage..."

Nicholas sure of himself said, "I know, actually, only handful of people are aware of this".

Unable to hide her excitement and curiosity, Kristen insisted, "Are you really sure? Whom did you learn this from?"

Nicholas' self-assuredness was reflected in his voice when he uncontrollably said, "If I weren't certain, I never would have said anything. And, this was a secret I wasn't supposed to reveal. But for some reason, I just wanted to tell you..." He also wanted add at the end of his sentence "… because I love you…", but he couldn't.

Kristen, as if wanting to demonstrate her continuing excited interest, said "Wonderful… You know what this means? This is something so incredible, it will kick off a new era".

Pleased with Kristen's opinion Nicholas added, "Zeugma means 'bridge', 'passage'. Once there was an arched Roman bridge which traversed the Euphrates. The town was named after this bridge. I think Leonardo was there and drew the bridge after seeing it. I think the grand master has coded in his works not mysteries, but rather things he was not allowed speak of or just couldn't reveal".

In contemplation, Nicholas took his mobile phone in silence. After a short struggle with the screen and choreographed dance of fingers, he smiled and handed the phone to Kristen. Excited with what she had been hearing, Kristen took the phone without realizing exactly why it was extended to her. Her eyes glued to the screen were opened wide. "I can't believe this, yes, of course, this is it... Incredible... Oh my God!" Amber jumped up "what is going on lady, let me take a look".

Nicholas had taken the photographs of the mosaic rendering at the Gaziantep Zeugma Mosaic Museum. Kristen was too excited to sit still. In excitement she said, "Nicholas, this is really amazing, please let me mention this to the professors at my school. Please?" Without giving it any thought Nicholas just said, "of course" and simultaneously a terrifying storm erupted in his soul: "What if the Man Carrying a Water Jug gets angry? What if he refuses to talk further?" These thoughts of severe doubt settled on him so suddenly, he was now clearly ill-at-ease and troubled.

"This is unbelievable. You are incredible. Hint me something you are not perfect in..." These sincere words of reflex loaded with feminine messages to Nicholas just dropped out of Kristen.

With her usual bluntness when Amber added, "now you are a perfect fit together" a sweet silence covered their dining table, all eyes evading one another. Kristen blushed a little. Quickly turned her head toward the beautiful mansions on the Bosphorus shore.

For an extended period they glued themselves to the marvelous scenery as the ship continued to glide on the Bosphorus. "How quickly time passed by..." were the words of Kristen as she looked with glittering eyes at the flowing current in the channel. As the ship took these three New Yorkers back to the European side of Istanbul, Nicholas was part happy and part sad. There was a short time left for Kristen's flight departure to America.

After deboarding the ship, he stopped a cab to take the girls to the airport. The car moving fast through sparkling evening city lights seemed to be taking his heart away with it. It was incredibly painful for him to wave Kristen goodbye. How could this be? Loving someone to death with such intensity and only in a brief period in a far away city?

Love! So unexpected, unknown and strangely powerful...

The cab he hired with sadness was now taking him to the hotel, but longing had already sunk in and was tearing his heart with devouring flames. Just as the Man Carrying a Water Jug had said: Longing hurts like the roots of pulled bundle of hair.

Clock was displaying 9:27 PM when he entered his room. He smiled without intent. Mumbled to himself "you, again?" and dropped his tired body on the bed. On the nights when he had the dream he always woke up at 03:27 AM. But since its first occurrence, this number always made its presence felt in his life. When he looked at the time, it was as if it stood there. When he finished a conversation, it seemed that's how long it took. When he bought his first car and made an accident he had seen that number on the calendar. He noticed it in the numbers of dead or wounded given in news casts. He seemed to be receiving messages on his phone at that time. Although initially he had paid little attention to this, eventually the number 27 became carved in his mind.

But now he was in no position to dwell on this subject. His heart was hurting, he was tired and what's more, the Man Carrying a Water Jug had commanded him saying, "be here at 03:27 AM". Actually he was very happy to have seen the glitter in Kristen's eyes. If eyes did not lie, then there was the possibility that she loved him, and this made Nicholas joyous. He set the alarm clock to 03:00 AM and closed his eyes.

It was incredible to see Hagia Sophia lit up in darkness and right in front of him when he opened his eyes. He felt as if he hadn't slept at all. He looked smiling at the dozen photographs of Kristen hanging on his room wall. These were the photos he had taken at their first coincidental meeting in Hagia Sophia. He was mesmerized and gazed at them with affection. Then at one moment he noticed the clock: 00:27...

He arose whispering, "You again?" This number meant something, but who was to know? He was still tired, but felt he had slept enough. The excitement of the upcoming encounter with the Old Man had already enveloped his entire body. Strangely, while with Kristen, he had forgotten all the mysteries and troublesome doubts gnawing his brain. Now, he was back in the same vortex again. He grabbed a cola from his refrigerator and stepped out to his balcony. Concerned, he took a few sips while looking at Hagia Sophia. It was a beautiful June night. Weather was warm. One could see easily from the sounds of the night that life was in full swing in the city. Not a single cloud in the dark sky. Moon appeared a little closer and a little larger. Full moon! He smiled when he thought, "my angel is flying to America at this very moment".

Full moon positioned above the Hagia Sophia added a unique flavor to the night with its glory. Since childhood, he always enjoyed the nights with full moon. He recalled his memories in Jacksonville where he climbed the roof of his house to look at the moon. Then as he sipped his cola, he suddenly remembered the words of the Man Carrying a Water Jug, "You will write in the book under moonlight only when the moon is full and clearly visible in the cloudless night, at times when the pen receives whole light. There shall not be any other light, only the moonlight..."

The old man said these when he handed over the book and the strange pen. Nicholas thought "why not?" and hastily went back into his room. Took out Leonardo's 'Book of Secrets' from his safe. Placed it on the balcony table. Quickly returned, turned off his room lights and brought back a glass of water. No light could possibly come from elsewhere to his upper floor room balcony. Only the moonlight lit the balcony. He thought this was a clever idea and concluded "if this book's writing had been supervised by the Old Man, then the same technique must have been used. Script written by a pen in need of full moonlight should also be readable under the same".

Carefully, he began sprinkling minute water droplets with his fingers to the pages. He continued for twenty or so pages, but the sparkling he anticipated on the script did not appear... Daunted, he kept whispering "this was a dumb idea". But he couldn't withhold himself from trying yet another page.

On the page he flipped last, suddenly a glitter occurred with the touch of a few droplets. A satisfying joy invaded him in a fraction of moment. He stood saying, "that's it, I got it". Writings began forming mysteriously among shimmering glitter but not like previously. Before, there was a white sparkling. But these were... blue.

Blue glittering sparks on and off at the top of the page became continuous light at the center and a fast ritual commenced. This was an indescribable sight. When the blue glittering finally ended a set of numbers became visible on the first line: 1,618033988749894… Immediately below it was written the "Law of Ratios". Some writings also appeared at the very bottom of the page: "In each and every opportunity you find, go afar, take a moment to contemplate, whence upon returning thou will have more decisive certainty. Be distant a little for troubles to diminish, thence thou shall overcome. What's lacking in harmony and ratio shall be self evident."

A picture familiar to Nicholas appeared above this writing. This picture would have been familiar to anyone interested in Leonardo Da Vinci's works. A circle and a square within which a nude male figure is positioned with arms and legs extended... Nicholas was unable not to murmur: "Vitruvian Man!!! Inspired by the famous Roman architect Marcus Vitruvius! The author of the famous *De Architectura*!!!"

Nicholas had learned of 'Vitruvian Man' when he investigated with curiosity the configuration given to the murdered museum director in that popular book *The Da Vinci Code* by Dan Brown.

He quickly flipped to the next page. Sprinkled a drop or two and a small green glitter appeared which did not dim quickly. Again, a new wonderful ceremony began. It was forming so fast, like a flood of green light covering the entire page. But, there appeared no writing at the end. Instead, it looked like a perfect sketch. No doubt, it was the sketch of the famous Mona Lisa. Absolutely… But, there seemed to be major differences. Nearly the whole world was in agreement that the Mona Lisa painting contained secrets and mysteries, and perhaps now all secrets were clearly in front of him. In Leonardo Da Vinci's own "Book of Secrets" which undoubtedly was like his personal memoir, in his own hand drawing...

A number '72' written in red was most evident on the bridge. In Mona Lisa's right eye was the characters 'VL'. In the left eye was the character 'B' written a little differently. It was something like a mixture of 'S' and 'B'. The entire sketch was on a fully black page and drawn in green. But, the characters in Mona's eyes and the number on the bridge were red colored. Additionally, one could see that Mona Lisa also had eyebrows which resembled that of mosaic female rendition excavated in Zeugma. Nicholas was very excited. His mind raced furiously, "Could it be that he was in possession of secrets wondered by so many? What could these characters and the number '72' inscribed on the bridge possibly imply?"

He flipped to the next page and gently sprinkled a few more little droplets. Writings began reappearing among red sparkles. He had to focus hard under the moonlight to be able to read. Script was in reverse, from right to left:

"Ceased his speech on women for a moment when he saw me examining the mosaics. I was looking at the eyes of the woman in the mosaic. They seemed alive and were looking back at me. He began to tell me about her. Next to her was King Solomon. It sounded like a legend. But, it did not matter, when King Solomon is involved, realities may have been legends and legends a reality. Did the woman in mosaic charm King Solomon as she bewitched me? That woman, Belkis, the mysterious angle of moon, perhaps Queen of Sheeba... who concubined with the King? But, he forbade me to ever mention her name. In fear of him I couldn't name my painting 'Belkis'. I, Leonardo, did not use my fingers or brushes like before. I finished it in the craze of full moons and in a manner befitting Belkis, the queen of the Moon. I never departed from it and always held it face up at each full moon..."

Nicholas bewildered with what he had been reading whispered to himself, "the male in the mosaic I thought to be Zeus may have been King Solomon". He hastily flipped another page. After a few more droplets of water, purple glitter appeared... and a little later, writings again:

"Belkis, princess of south and queen of the mysterious Moon. When she entered worldly life, she was a female child with long hair and eye lashes. She was so beautiful, those who saw her once could not turn for a second look. She had a blinding light kneaded with purity. Contrary to physical beauty attributed to her in tales, it was actually an abstract, intangibly distant but admirably effective light. Without anyone could realize, she formed her rule over the land here. It was here, around this river, a kingdom feared by many. Belkis, the mysterious princess of the south, sacrificed everything for love. King Solomon's love... Solomon gave his love, but in return removed all power from her and her kingdom. Then, Belkis annulled her agreement. Turned her back to those on the Moon. And I made her painting to be near them. I kept the painting with me years on end, faced it up to the full moon and touched it time after time so that I may speak to them, reach the secrets. Oh, Belkis!... the little devil!..."

What could Da Vinci be possibly hinting at with these strange words? Nicholas, anxious to find answers jumped at the next page and repeated the ritual. This time around white sparkles began shedding light but writings appeared slowly:

"Those in Florence make inventions. But none works in reality. All on paper. I try with all my might to realize them. But not enough time. The carrier of the jug showed me strange things. I wondered what they may be, but he didn't even answer. Said that these were not my concern. Mentioned someone called Isaac. Said that those belonged to him. In front of my eyes, he mixed three liquids and poured it on the grape leaves. It was wonderful. It steamed and the wine leaf turned into gold. I begged him but he said it belongs to Isaac. Whoever that might be? Later I spoke of this to a friend, he warned me to stay away saying, 'it must be alchemy'. I looked everywhere for the Jug Carrier but couldn't find him. Thus I went to those who had offered treaty to Belkis. I reflected her light truly under the moonlight. I held it up to the moon so they may speak to me. I've never kept it apart from me."

What could all this mean? Nicholas was awed. Da Vinci had used the book like his diary. It was difficult to assign a meaning to what he was expressing. Were there people on the moon, why would he say 'those on the moon'? Was such a master stuck in a legend, a tale? If he held up the portrait at each full moon, did he believe he might actually be able to talk to them? Did he mean some other secret with the word 'moon'? Who really was this woman called 'Belkis"? What did Da Vinci exactly mean when he said 'little devil'? Nicholas' mind was now thoroughly mixed up.

He flipped another page. In confusion, he sprinkled a few more droplets. But no such luck… Nothing happened. At that moment he suddenly felt sorrow. Moved to the next page hoping for another miracle. To no avail. Another 20 or so pages yielded no glitter or shimmer. He abandoned the balcony table feeling very down.

A deep curiosity surrounded him. He mumbled to himself whisperingly, "Surely he must have revealed all his secrets in this book. Probably, in the remaining pages".

In order to read the remaining pages he clearly needed the Man Carrying a Water Jug as stated by Da Vinci in very beginning of the book. He thought, "all this was discovered by his clever approach, but if it weren't for the Old Man who warned of writings which would appear in full moon, none could have conceived such a thing".

As Nicholas contemplated the numbers and characters visible in the Mona Lisa sketch, he was also gazing at the moon which shed incredible beauty to Istanbul. He kept repeating the questions, "Who is Belkis, Princess of the South? Did he mean something else when he said 'the moon'?" In reality he was only trying to occupy himself and avoid the fear as well as anxiety of his fast approaching encounter with the Old Man. Absorbed in million thoughts, and as he was gazing at the glittering city, felt his sight frozen suddenly. The sip he had taken from his flat and warm cola stuck in his mouth. He quickly sat down in front of the book. Reexamining the Mona Lisa sketch he almost screamed, "of course...." he said, "Da Vinci writes in reverse... from right to left". This was the unchanging rule for the master of mysteries in disguising secrets. Thus, this meant the characters 'VL' in Mona's right eye stood for 'LV' which were the initials of his name. And, the character appearing as a mixture of 'S' and 'B' in the left eye was the initial of Belkis mentioned by Da Vinci as the Princess of South. Accordingly, '72' on the bridge stood for '27'. Nicholas was now numbed and glued stiff on his balcony chair. Distant early morning sounds of the city throbbed in his ear drums.

He was in agony at the clawed hands of strange feelings as he left the hotel. The scripts which appeared in the book had confused him sufficiently. Wasn't Da Vinci a master of mysterious paintings? But, it was clear that he had gone through even deeper mysteries which he could not reveal. Possibly some similar to Nicholas' mysterious circumstances and events of late. Short notes in Da Vinci's diary brought forward new secrets for Nicholas who had already been immersed in the unknown far too long. In the darkness he looked once again at his wrist watch: 03:20 AM. With fear ridden doubts erupting in his heart, he anxiously quickened his steps toward Hagia Sophia. All was quite in the vicinity. Not a single soul on the streets.

"The only problem…" he thought, "…is him saying he is the Man Carrying Water. How could he be alive in this century? Could it be the Templar Knights? How about Sion? It can't be... There is a dream which has been recurring for years. No secret organization can incept a dream always at the same time. But, how did he manage to live so long? Possible?"

His mind was agonizing as if he had fallen in a dark endless labyrinth. Finally, after a brief brisk walk he was at the bolted iron gate of Hagia Sophia garden.

"Welcome Mr. Nicholas…" Familiar voice came from the dark. Moments later he saw the butler who had led him in previously emerge from darkness. Lowering his head in salutation, the butler politely acknowledged him and gestured a gentle invitation for entry into the temple garden. Led by him, Nicholas walked quietly and submissively. The ritual was repeated. The big temple gate was opened, Nicholas stepped in, the robed butler closed the door behind and disappeared. One unexpected difference stood out shockingly clear. The Man Carrying a Water Jug who had been on his feet right beneath the massive temple chandelier in the center stepped forward with agility and visible sincerity toward Nicholas and gave him an affectionate hug saying, "Nicholas… Welcome…"

Nicholas was standing in front of the Old Man with a soldierly respect amidst a whirlpool of emotions kneaded with fear, trepidation and curiosity. "Did you see Kristen off?", this question posed by the Old Man hinted at an intend to calm Nicholas. Nicholas stuttered "yye… yess… she left this evening".

They were now in front of the massive door said to be a remainder of Noah's Ark. Old Man turned his back to Nicholas, took a few steps, stopped suddenly and leant forward to the floor. Interior of the temple flooded with noise. This temple with incredible acoustic at night silence echoed violently even by a step taken, let alone an iron lid lifted from the ancient marble flooring. Noise was caused by the iron lid when the Old Man pulled it open. He looked at Nicholas with piercing eyes and a smile said, "Don't worry, those organizations which concerned you on your way here mean nothing in my domain". Clearly this was a response to thoughts Nicholas had only a short while ago. Hearing these words left Nicholas in the midst of indecision, he didn't know if he should be glad or more troubled. Not only he was almost totally numb when near the Old Man, but his thoughts from a few minutes ago being responded to was scary to say the least. He couldn't help thinking, "He is reading my mind…"

The Old Man knelt down and carefully sat on the marble edge of the manhole entrance revealed by the lifted iron lid. He slowly and silently slid in. Then his voice, as if arising from a water well, was heard echoing above, "Nicholas! Aren't you coming?"

As if to acknowledge a command, "…excuse me, right away.." he answered immediately, but he was afraid. When he stood for a moment at the edge of the manhole iron lid, he saw the stairs going downward. He began stepping down in fear and was unable to control the trembling of his legs. He thought, "what am I doing... have I gone out of mind?" but incapable of any logic and unable to control any emotions, he was being drawn downward. It was a long way down. At the bottom of stairs below he walked through a narrow corridor at the end of which the Old Man was in sight. He thought he was smelling the aroma of seashore or sea weeds. The interior of the surrounding walls appeared quite damp. Upon reaching the location of the Old Man through the passage, he was confronted with a mind boggling incredible sight. They were at a fairly dim place. Lights were at a distance. An enormous pool and beautiful still water stood in front of him. Beneath the temple was a reservoir as far as the eye can see. He estimated it to be at least 30-40 ft below the temple floor. A little ahead were several dozens of rotten wooden pieces which undoubtedly were once parts of small boats. This was unbelievable. Lake-like scenery and boats under such a temple. Then he noticed what appeared to be floating old canteens. This scene reminded him of a paragraph which he had read while researching Hagia Sophia. It claimed that shortly after the 1915 War of Gallipoli and Dardanelles, the British army contingency soldiers stationed in Istanbul, stepped all over each other and entered into violent fist fights in a rush to fill their canteens with the Holy Water. Nicholas thought that "these canteens must have fallen into the pool at that time and been floating ever since".

The Old Man finally ended his silence and commented: "This is a cistern which collects the rain water falling on Hagia Sophia. Watch your step. It is very slippery. Just follow me". Nicholas faithfully did as he was told, followed each step as they walked adjacent to the chamber wall. A little ahead where their path ended, the Old Man stopped facing a wall and filled a small bowl with water from his jug which he never seemed to keep distant. He sprinkled water at the wall from the bowl. Repeated the ritual three times. A door sized portion of the wall became visibly wet. Nicholas just observed without any comprehension. Then the Old Man forced this wet wall part forward. When he pushed a little harder the door sized portion slid backward with noise drowning the entire cistern chamber. A section barely man sized opened. First the Old Man, then Nicholas stepped through this tight passage to the other side. It was very dim. Sharp sea weed aroma and heavy smell of damp walls dominated the darkness. A short walkway quickly turned into a sharp incline of narrow stepped stair downward.

Nicholas just followed with anxiety and sense of discovery, all the while with new questions pouring in. The journey down seemed endless. Not knowing where they were headed in a strange place like this added great apprehension. Soon enough stairs ended abruptly and a flat, narrow floored, low ceilinged, dungeon-like passage took Nicholas finally to a place full of amazement and wonder.

No longer dim, it appeared as if he was on the shore of a large lake. Walls had cartouches, some in the form of lion, tiger and chimera with water flowing from their mouths. Water poured into the pool. There were dozens of them. The ceiling was very high.

They were at a place which covered an area larger than that of the temple above. There were no columns holding the ceiling.

There were three small boats ahead of them with magnificent wooden carvings resembling royalty boats. The Old Man still holding the jug headed to third one on the right. He boarded it slowly, took the throne-like seat, and gestured with his hand at Nicholas to take the opposite one. Utterly surprised with what he was experiencing, Nicholas also boarded the boat which seemed better decorated than the others. Curious enough, same gilding on the glass pen given to him the other day by the Old Man seemed also to be part of this boat's ornamentation. As Nicholas took the opposite seat, the Old Man poured water from his jug to the cup and emptied it into a square hole located on the side of the boat. After carefully placing the jug near him, he lifted a thin iron bar located at the edge of square hole. At that moment the boat began moving slowly forward. Nicholas had million questions, but Leonardo Da Vinci had forbidden asking questions in his diary by saying "do not question him, otherwise the journey will end". Nicholas once tried questioning and the response was "no question-answer dialogue, you must resolve them during your journey". The boat was moving alright but there were no sounds of anything like a motor. The only sounds around came from the waterfall like pouring out of the wall figurine mouths. The Old Man was silently observing the water. Nicholas' curious eyes were on everything which surrounded him.

The boat slowly approached the area where there seemed to be more light. As the chamber became more lit, with widened eyes in amazement and wonder, Nicholas had no choice but to be further absorbed in the surrounding scenery. Walls had hieroglyphics of the ancient Egypt. He had visited Egypt three times. What he was seeing now was just like those he had observed not only in Egypt but also in the American and British museums. So much so that he couldn't help but wonder whether he was in "Egypt, Istanbul? Inside the Ghiza Pyramid or Hagia Sophia temple?"

As he was viewing a goddess figurine with both arms stretched and with wings attached which resembled that of an eagle, hieroglyphics of birds accompanying her, the Old Man suddenly commented: "Those who do not know the history of Istanbul can never know the history of Egypt".

Nicholas failed to see the connection. He wanted to ask but he couldn't. The Old Man uttered a single sentence and returned to his silence. He had also failed on the day of his arrival in Istanbul to assign a meaning to the Amon Ra column brought to the Sultanahmet Square and continued to stand there for centuries. In one of the biggest empires built by the Turks, why would a remnant silhouette of a civilization which totally fell opposite to the Islamic concepts be brought to the capital city of the Ottoman Empire, not to mention to the most important square next to the Palace? This was another mystery for him.

Silent motion of the boat continued. Upon arrival to the brighter section where more water seemingly poured out, Nicholas was completely mesmerized in adoration and nearly frozen in wonderment. He recognized immediately the large goddess figurine in front of him. This was Nefertiti and she was holding a water jug in her hand. Water pouring from the chamber wall was entering into the mouth of the jug in her hand. When the top jug was filled, water from a hole on it, filled the two below. From there water continued to the cistern pool. Water did not pour continuously. It stopped intermittently.

The Old Man's voice awakened him from this mesmerizing scene and Nicholas looked at him obediently. "This is an Egyptian clepsydra used to measure time. The phrase, 'time flows like water' originates from this". Then the Old Man reached out and pulled down the thin iron bar stopping the boat right in front of the clepsydra. Opened a small cupboard on the side of his seat. Pulled out a plate with cubic morsels of food on it. Affectionately extended the plate to Nicholas offering him to taste some. Nicholas took one respectfully. This was not something he had tasted before. It was delicious. It just dissolved in his mouth leaving a pleasant after taste. It was sweet. Having taken one himself, the Old Man continued, "This is made with sesame oil called *tahini*. You must always have a little bit after eating food. It is extremely beneficial. Later I will tell you all about it. It will add a lot to your life", and offered more to Nicholas. This time around Nicholas was quick to say "with pleasure, Sir" and enjoyed it. After placing the plate in the cupboard, the Old Man lifted the iron bar and again the boat moved forward silently.

Just as they passed the clepsydra, the sharp coarse voice of the Old Man echoed:

"Water... water... so abundant and common, yet so mysterious. It is with us in every moment of our lives. Do we know the secrets of this magnificent creation? Where did it come from? The amount of water on and in the world never changes significantly, if you discount the unappreciated amounts disrespectfully polluted and rendered unfit for all God's creatures for the last two centuries by your spoiled grandfathers in haste, this miracle is otherwise in gentle and loving balance... like God's even hand in universe". As he spoke, like a playful but reserved child adoring water, he dipped his hand from the boat side, took a palmful and rubbed his face. He did this exactly three times. Then he continued with the same ritual like play, only this time, he was releasing the water back to the pool. He kept looking at the water with adoration and added:

"In this World, there exists nothing which is softer and submissive than water and yet capable of abrading, chiseling seemingly infinite hardness. Nothing can overcome water but nothing is more easily had. Strange, isn't it?"

There was a moment of silence. Nicholas was listening intently. He felt the moment he had been waiting finally arrived. The word "water" was written on the rear of each page in Leonardo Da Vinci's 'Book of Secrets'. The gilded book became readable only after water droplets sprinkled prior to the dance of glitters. Leonardo da Vinci had imagined various water utilizing devices. These were hydrolic devices. Nicholas knew that the rich American Bill Gates had purchased them for incredible sums, and concluded, "Eventually I'll learn the reasons behind Leonardo's great interest in water". The Old Man's brief silence ended while he was caressing and dipping his hand into the pool, raising bird-chirp like playful foreground water sounds occasionally emerging from the humming and roaring of the surrounding waterfalls, and causing on the dark water surface ever widening, silvery crested and gleaming concentric gentle waves which, Nicholas thought, were soothing and hypnotic:

"Do you know, son? People are not aware of water's importance. If they had known even just a little what diseases lack of water causes, they would have been terrified. So many ailments… So much grief. No water no joy, no life. Death everywhere… Look into it. Most ailments known since ancient times to your era can be traced down to either lack of pure, heavenly clean water, or to polluted, filthy water."

Nicholas burst in amazement, "lack of water in the body is the cause of many ailments?"

The Old Man gazed cold at the water he was playing with, "Unfortunately!" Then he fixed his eyes on Nicholas. Within a moment that gentle smile resettled on his face. Secretive sentences followed again:

"Water is known to have unequalled characteristics. Unlike other substances, when frozen for example, it expands. In your era, men of knowledge understood the pressure which could be generated by water in the body. Did you not notice? A seed in soil expands when the right time comes. Some even push apart the hard surface. Water causes all of this. How does a minute quantity create such a great impact? This is a very special feature unique to water. Hardly any other substance exhibits such a character. If water did not have this miracle, there would have been no life on Earth. Water is endowed with miracles. Water is unequalled. It is the essence of life!"

These were very interesting indeed. Nicholas had not given much thought to these matters previously. If he was ever asked, his most likely answer might have been "well...water... is water". He lowered his head as if wanting not to disrupt the Old Man. The coarse sharp voice echoed almost scarily in the acoustic chamber:

"Why water is the liquid with the highest surface tension? Why water is the mighty dissolver of most substances? And why does it rise so high easily in the trunks and branches of trees?"

Nicholas was awed as the Old Man hinted knowledge of modern science. It also appeared as if he was being informed through the ancient Socrates method. He felt the Old Man was not really asking questions but rather trying to insert the secrets in his mind with questions posed. Hushing his penetrating voice a little, the Old Man added:

"Think of the opening passage of the Holy Bible... Creation is primarily related to water".

These words struck Nicholas' mind like a lightning in a dark storm. "Yes", he thought, opening sentences of the Bible and Da Vinci's "Book of Secrets". Now he related better to all.

When the Old Man turned the thin iron bar sideways, the boat began turning toward their point of embarkation. As the boat reoriented itself, he continued:

"Your world... my world... is a massive reservoir of water which incubated all life forms. Beware that each creature whether alive or not, is itself a reservoir of water. Now, some seek water first at distant cosmic, heavenly bodies among the stars. WATER!"

"No water, no life!"

The Old Man appeared to hint at higher knowledge of current science when he referred to basic building blocks of life and water's relation to existing life. Clearly he was in the know. "How could this be?" thought Nicholas, utterly shocked.

Nicholas was mesmerized as it is with Egypt in the midst of Istanbul, but what he was told about water and its significance happened to be the last drop fueling his drunkenness. No longer apprehensive, and fairly comforted, he couldn't help but amuse himself: "I'll write *Nicholas in Wonderland*". Meanwhile, the Old Man was scanning the walls in contemplation and silence, as if to permit Nicholas to absorb all in small intervals. Thoughts raced in the young man's mind. Indeed, this was a journey in an ancient land of mysteries and exquisite tales of knowledge.

As the boat neared others parked, he heard the Old Man saying:

"Special antibacterial water was used recently in Afghanistan and Iraq. All around the world people believe in the miracles of some types of water. Did you ever hear of *zhemzhem*? Did you ever wonder why some ancient peoples in Asia, like the ancestors of present day Turks or their ancient relatives in America, never harmed water, creeks, rivers or lakes? Do you know what Turks have been saying for thousands of years to those who offer water to thirsty ones? '*May you have long life as water*!' Why ancient

Egyptians so revered water in addition to Nile's cyclical flooding of crop lands? Do you know, for example, some illiterates among our *own* believed and still believe that water blessed by some priests never molds! This of course is due to airtight containers not permitting any interaction with another essential ingredient of life, the air! Surely, you must know of *baptising*, done only with water?"

Nicholas was shocked. Especially by the reference to Afghan and Iraq wars. He was an American but he hadn't heard of the antibacterial water used by the soldiers. The Old Man was fully aware of what has been transpiring in the world.

When their boat joined the others, the Old Man slowly stepped out first. Nicholas followed. Many questions were lined up in his mind. As they began walking back he kept listening attentively.

"Somewhere in the South East Asia... Year 1956..."

The Old Man stopped for a moment as if to catch his breath. Then proceeded while speaking:

"A military laboratory where weapons of mass destruction were developed and produced. A new generation bacteriological weapon was being researched. During a secret meeting all participants suffered a sudden attack of debilitating pain, everyone was floored. Investigations done at the hospitals revealed no results. The scientists had consumed nothing but water in the meeting room. The water was tested but nothing was found. But they reported '*water poisoning*' anyway. Let me give you a vital secret Nicholas. Water absorbs external influences, assumes their characteristics. It transforms itself. This is a very unique specialty of water. This is an important secret of water. Think on this most carefully..."

Stairs climbing up were conquered. Nicholas, too, was tired. Finally they reached the very first cistern chamber. The Old Man repeated the original ritual, but this time by wetting the base of an opening in the wall. The opening reslit shut to its initial position. It only appeared as a damp wall with no trace of ever having been passed through. All of a sudden, there was no physical evidence of what had transpired for the last hour or more. They left the cistern area with slow and careful steps through the same walkway. The Old Man was silent again. A silence which did not invite any questions and which left Nicholas hopelessly helpless in view of numerous questions yet unanswered. Surprising for his unknown old age, The Man Carrying a Water Jug reached quickly the manhole entrance on the floor of Hagia Sophia. What really got the best of Nicholas was the extended hand offering help to the young man for climbing out of darkness and mystery. It was like a metaphor depicting years of confusion, fear and intense curiosity which occupied Nicholas. *A mysterious and loving Old Man extending a helping hand to pull a young man out of his predicament.* When Nicholas grabbed the hand offered, he felt no bones. In the blink of an eye and so effortlessly he was back on the temple floor next to the manhole. The Old Man easily closed the entrance with the iron lid. Everything seemed to have occurred and evaporated in an instant. Nicholas was back to where he was initially. Standing erect in full respect and apprehension. The Old Man touched his shoulder in a fatherly manner and said: "Now go to your hotel, eat, drink your water. Tomorrow night, be here exactly at 03:27. After eating today, do not eat or drink a drop of water. Go around all day long, visit Bosphorus, run a little. And while doing all of that contemplate why a bowl might be holy. Is it because of the person drinking from it? Or because of its content? Might itself be holy?"

The first lights of dawn were striking Istanbul. The man who had met him at night accompanied him once again to the exit and said goodbye. On the Sultan Ahmed Square no one else but the municipal cleaners were present. He felt as if he had drunk a generous shot of whisky. What he had seen during the night, heard and experienced was dazzling. Not fully aware what to make of it all, his mind struggling with questions, he walked slowly from Sultanahmet towards his hotel with hands in his pockets.

Pleasantly smiling, the receptionist handed him over the room card. Nicholas returned the smile and headed for the elevator. But, instead of his room he preferred the top floor restaurant. Asked for a hot lentil soup and disregarding the hour of dawn he ordered without thinking the recommended Topkapı dish which had been a delight previously. The headwaiter, now almost fully familiar with Nicholas' odd dining hours, suggested with affection, "May I also offer you a nice seasonal salad on the side, Mr. Nicholas?" Pleased, he smiled back at his attentive waiter and said, "fine".

Having lunch instead of breakfast was a little strange. But, he was up and about after a short nap since the very early hours of the morning, and not having had anything to eat, for him it seemed as if a full day. Just a coke, and yes, two pieces of that pleasant dessert which the Old Man had offered to him in front of the Clepysdra, saying "this is a desert made with *tahini*. You must always have some after dinner. Incredibly useful. In times ahead I'll tell you about its benefits and explain how it is made. It extends your lifetime..." He had an unbelievable adventure the entire night. Now it felt not like the initial hours of the morning, but rather like the mid-day. Not only that, but he was instructed by the Old Man to eat and drink water, and fast until the next midnight. Nicholas hadn't comprehended this fully, but he knew he had to obey. Time till next midnight was not short and he thought it was wise to eat heartily, and this was just the dish needed.

First the delicious soup, then the Topkapı, a famous Turkish palace dish, served with rice pilaf mixed in variety of spices and rolled in chicken leg meat ball, with a delicious sauce atop. Regardless the strange hour, he was experiencing such delicious food for the first time.

A well-brewed dark Turkish tea was a must after such a delicious meal. None could possibly betray this engrained ancient tradition. Certainly not in an early hazy Istanbul morning. As he sipped the hot tea and looked at Hagia Sophia with excitement, he was juggling in his mind the previous evening's secretive scripts revealed in Da Vinci's 'Book of Secrets', all that went on in the Temple, and all the mysterious information given by the Old Man. No one could possibly believe what had been going on. He thanked and tipped the waiter, headed to his room on the floor below. He was tired. But now, sleeping didn't seem possible.

Even though a puzzle, he would spend his whole day around Bosphorus as instructed after eating and drinking water. But not a morsel of food and not a drop of water the whole day. All the time he was thinking what was said by the old man with a water jug. He already had been immersed in what was said ever since the words were uttered by the mysterious Old Man.

Upon arrival at his room, he headed to the shower. A warm shower was the best way to melt away his exhaustion. As if to find an answer, he was thinking aloud under the water: "Why would a cup be holly? Is it because of the liquid it contains? Or, is the cup itself?"

A short while later, comforted, he stepped out of shower, but he was as confused as ever. Grabbed the water bottle from his small cooler, sipped a couple of drops. Strangely, this time the water tasted very pleasant. He drank more to quench his thirst, but to no avail, with every gulp he felt even thirstier. All the while, what the Old Man had said during the night was racing through his mind. After every sip he kept looking at the water in the bottle. "How strange, it has no color, no smell and no taste" he thought. He took another chilled bottle from the cooler and dropped himself to the couch. As he continued to sip slowly, he was looking at Kristen's pictures on the wall while his mind was preoccupied with the holy cup.

He rose suddenly, sat at the table. Turned on his computer and began to note down the events of the last little while. He felt he needed to share certain things with someone. It just didn't seem possible to resolve these mysteries single-handedly. He would have felt more at ease if he could have resolved the identity of the Old Man. The idea of a Man Carrying a Water Jug at the time of Jesus was strange as it is. There were many centuries in between. How could he have met today a man who lived at the time of Jesus? This was impossible. Even so, who was this man? There were no logical answers. He was irritated. He felt he had to tell someone the details of all this. Obviously, to no one else but his dear friend Michael…

He wrote everything in great detail. At the bottom he added, "The Old Man asked me: Why is a cup holy? Is it because of its content or because of who drinks from it? Is it because of the liquid in it? Michael, what do you think about this? Call me!" He sent the email.

While writing about what had occurred earlier he kept drinking water. The fifth bottle was in his hand and he was full. He began dressing to step out. As he combed his hair, his eyes on the mirror shone involuntarily. He mumbled excitedly, "This is an organization… Opus Dei or Sion, or whatever the hell they are… They sure got the holy cup, the Holy Grail, otherwise, why mention it? Why ask about it?" This was Nicholas' thinking aloud technique which he used to develop his advertisement ideas and slogans, talking in front of a mirror alone in a room. But, the glamour in his eyes disappeared at once as he mumbled again, "Stop this nonsense Nicholas, even that was so, why should he tell you, what's so special about you? Are you the Pope or something?" He smiled hopelessly and dashed out of the room.

For a visit, the first place that occurred to him was the ancient obelisk he had seen several days ago and learned much about. His steps were decisive, but his mind was nowhere near. He began walking by the tramway near the Sultan Ahmet Square or the Hippodrome of Constantinople as called in the Byzantine era. Soon enough he was at the several thousand years old obelisk which had been standing there for the last several centuries. Tourists were already crowding its surrounding. He was more excited now in front of this erect monolith than the first time he had seen it. To take a closer look, he moved in among the tourist crowd.

"Nothing is obvious, but something must have happened here, right here…" were the words spilled out of him inadvertently, causing the old couple in front of him glimpse back in curiosity. The elderly tourist gentleman smiled warmly and said "Yes, young man, at this very place, Christianity was declared no longer forbidden. Oppressions and persecutions were over… Jesus' dream was realized here…" Nicholas returned the smile.

This monolithic rock, unknown to most passersby, was in a way a personal witness to what one might call Christianity's Declaration of Freedom. Nicholas paced slowly around the rock obelisk with a strange feeling. Due to the great efforts of the Byzantine Emperor Constantine I's mother Helena, Christianity was declared free and the declaration was read personally by the Emperor at the base of this obelisk known as the Constantine Column located at center of the Constantine Forum. This declaration of freedom was made at the base of this very monolith now known as the Hooped Rock. This legalization was welcomed with great happiness by the Christians. Church constructions at many locales of the city followed it.

After the declaration of Christianity free by the Roman Empire, Helena had practiced her long hidden religion more openly, got permission from her son the Emperor, and went to Jerusalem for an extensive visit. Having started her journey in 325 AD, she reached Jerusalem in the year 326 AD. Staying in Jerusalem for nearly two years, Helena departed for Istanbul in 328 AD and carried with her numerous holy artifacts. Among the artifacts treasure brought was a grail which contained no inscription other than the letters X and P.

With the arrival of those holy artifacts, Constantinople assumed an even more significant place among the Christians.

When the calendar showed the year 1204AD, a call issued by the Pope Innocentius the Third invited all Christians to unite for Jerusalem. This was clearly a call for a Crusade. This was met with joy by the Christians. The fourth Crusader army of 1204 was successful on the second attack to the city and occupied it. Yes, this is what the history books wrote. The crusader army headed for Jerusalem actually attacked Constantinople. The Crusades had been organized against the Muslims and had the objective of recapturing Jerusalem. But, the 1204 Crusades had set the goal of capturing Constantinople, the heart of the Byzantine where Christianity had been declared free. History books particularly noted the pillaging and plunder done in Hagia Sophia.

Until 1261, when Mikhail Palaiologos the 8th recaptured Istanbul, the city remained under the control of the Crusaders and the city was completely plundered. Much of what had been stolen was brought to the Vatican and others were distributed within Europe. Undoubtedly, among the most valuable artifacts plundered were the relics brought by Helena from Jerusalem. One of the items was a piece of the Holy Cross currently displayed at Santa Groce Basilica.

Nicholas, having recalled this information from the history books, once again thinking aloud, he mumbled, "Why the hell did they do this to a Christian city? Were they nuts, why did they plunder it?" The man standing next to him extended a hand while saying to Nicholas, "Why? My friend, the Templars were looking for the Holy Grail, it too was here at that time…" Nicholas, smiling, shook the hand. He began chatting with this man who identified himself as Jean. Jean was French and a professor of history. The short chat was filled with incredibly surprising information. Tourist group was getting ready to move on to another historical site, he bid farewell to Jean indicating to meet again. With unusual feelings churning in him, Nicholas also left the Hooped Rock.

He was returning from the same road to head for the Bosphorus as he repeated what was said by the professor from France. "Yes, my friend, this grail is an unbelievable thing, a Christian crusader army attacked Byzantium, another Christian country, for this grail. Without any pity, they pillaged and plundered the city and Hagia Sophia. For sure, they knew that the Holy Grail was at Hagia Sophia. But they couldn't find it. Beneath the Hagia Sophia were numerous galleries and tunnels woven like a labyrinth. They stayed in the city for many years, they delivered everything they could find to the Vatican. The only thing they couldn't locate was that grail"…

Nicholas arrived at the Sultan Ahmet Square and followed the curving tramway near the Hagia Sophia downward towards the Bosphorus with familiar questions on his mind…

"Thirty million dollars… Consider it well and please be quick about it. My client is very sensitive on this matter."

The smiling young man at the end of the luxurious table was now taking another sip from his drink in the comfort of conviction that his offer was a very generous one.

"Ali, I will pass on your proposal to my friend. It is a generous offer, I hope to reach an agreement. But of course you must give me a little time. I spoke with the professor Alexander only about a book which we have. You reached me through the professor, so your proposal was unexpected. My friend will be back home within a week or two, we will consider your offer, we haven't considered its sale before," said Michael.

The young man appeared to be perturbed by the fact that he was a director of a well known auction house while he said, "Do not rush your decision. This is not an offer that can be rejected easily… I must reemphasize that I am not here on behalf of the auction house where I work. This is only about a personal business acquaintance expressing an interest in the lost codex of Leonardo Da Vinci. My company is not involved. I am here on behalf of a friend."

"Mr. Ali, there is someone on the phone for you, it is reforwarded from the lobby sir…" was the interruption by the young, gently speaking Press Lounge waiter. When Ali politely excused himself from the table to take the call saying "with your permission…", Michael focused at the magnificent panorama of New York facing him, he was excited by the thirty million dollar proposal.

They were at the reputed top floor Press Lounge on the 11th Avenue. From the 48th floor, it boasted a great view of the New York City. Clearly, its popularity came primarily from this panorama.

In order to help out his buddy, Michael had spoken with the art professor Alexander Keyes at the university indicating to him that, "we have a book in our hand claimed to have been written by Da Vinci". He was extremely careful not uttering a word about or hinting that Nicholas dug it out in Jerusalem.

He spoke of Da Vinci's 'Book of Secrets' as "an old leather-bound book among others purchased from a respected Istanbul bibliopole by a friend." It was an innocent white lie spoken for Nicholas' and his own security. The professor was very interested and inquired about the book. He wanted to know about the shape of the word 'water' inscribed on all pages, the introductory statements at the beginning of the book, and the details of Hagia Sophia picture drawn on the final page. Strange enough, the phone call he received the next day got him to the Press Lounge where he was now.

The voice on the line had said, "Hello… This is Ali Ertuğrul. I am an auction house director. Professor Alexander Keyes is a close friend of mine. He mentioned a book to me. Michael, a Leonardo da Vinci admirer businessman friend of mine has been collecting his books for many years. I have an offer you won't be able to refuse. Tomorrow evening let us meet at the Press Lounge and talk about this subject over dinner. If you agree, I'll be very appreciative…" Now, Michael was at the 48th floor quite pleased and viewing the panorama.

When Ali returned a little while later smiling, he politely said as he was being reseated, "I apologize, when you have private clients, day or night makes no difference, we are at work at every hour of the day."

After an exquisite but obviously expensive dinner in the Press Lounge, they were enjoying their drinks. Ali was a Turk who had studied in the US and was a successful auction house manager who had been living in the States for a long time. Michael had seen his name several times in the newspapers. He was a well-off manager who was seen frequently in the art world and receptions.

Although Ali tried to establish a closer dialogue through references to the magnificent night lights of the city and funny events of various auctions, he did not neglect bringing the subject to the 'Book Of Secrets'. It was obvious that he wanted to collect as much information as possible.

When he said things like, "Michael, what other things concerning water are there in the book in addition to the background inscription 'water'?", he was obviously desiring to learn more.

As if wanting to better understand the details of Ali's enquiry, Michael retorted, "what do you mean?"

Ali, having taken another sip from his drink, moved closer to the table.

"Well, it could be the drawings of discoveries concerning water, or, well.... how should I say, it could be an incredible writing about water, maybe even, it might be a disclosure about the location of a water source. Well, after all, we are talking about Da Vinci, aren't we?"

Nicholas hadn't provided much detail on the book anyway. Michael spoke with the hardship of very limited knowledge, "I don't know the details at the moment. My friend is there on an advertisement project. It's difficult to communicate with him at times like this. I don't really know the contents of the book."

Ali's face took on a more serious expression.

"Michael, I'll be very frank with you. If the book contains strange drawings about water or if there are descriptions of a water source, my client is ready to renew his offer."

A fairly experienced ad man, knowing that the figure will rise, looked at Ali with inquiring eyes and asked, "what kind of a renewal?".

"If the book contains what I just mentioned, he is ready to pay fifty million dollars. In fact, if it includes information about a water source, I'll speak to him, and I am sure he will raise the figure. "

With excitement of the amount mentioned, words dropped out of Michael, "Well, like I said before, I don't have much knowledge about the content, but I can tell you that initially the book had blank pages but when Nicholas, while playing with his wet hair after a shower, accidentally dropped a water droplet on it, the inscriptions appeared with glitters. The things which appeared were all about water. I think the book might contain what you are looking for."

Ali suddenly moved even closer to the table. Excitedly he asked, "Michael are you really sure, did the inscriptions appear with a water droplet?"

Michael responded with a little reservation, "Yes, it was a book with dark pages initially, but inscriptions were revealed with a water droplet."

Ali's face acquired a teasing smirk. It wasn't hard to read the joy in his eyes. It was as if he had finally heard what he wanted to hear. Like a hunter who caught a great prey, he leaned back at ease in his comfortable chair.

Ali was a fairly happy guy who knew well how to affect a person. He was one of those characters who attracted all the attention around him when he spoke. He had quite a charismatic personality. The Press Lounge waiters spinned around the table all night long and at Ali's slightest glimpse, they delivered excellent service to the table. It was obvious that Ali was a regular and an important guest. The time had flown by with expensive drinks and funny stories of auctions. Michael looked at his watch and said, "Wow, its 1 AM already, I have no idea how time passed by, tomorrow I have meetings, with your permission, I should head home".

Ali stood up very politely and accompanied his guest to the elevator. Ali, touching at Michael's shoulder affectionately, said "I am now quite sure we will reach an understanding, but let me say it again, if there are other writings in it about water, it's fifty million, but if there are references to a source, we will carry the figure higher." Michael replied, "Once Nicholas returns, I'll introduce you to him and I think we'll reach an agreement." He smiled, said goodbye and entered the elevator. Just as he reached the hotel lobby on the 11th Avenue, his mobile phone indicated the arrival of a message, the screen was lit reading 'Nico'. For a brief instant he wondered why he might have messaged him at a very odd hour, but just as quickly he recalled the time zone difference between New York and Istanbul. Smiling he thought, "now… morning in Istanbul". As he stepped out of the hotel, he opened the message. He was surprised to see that it was actually a long e-mail.

"Good evening, Sir, would you care for a cab?" was the voice of the hotel doorman. While Michael's eyes were on the screen, he replied "Yes, please". He got in the cab and started to read Nicholas' e-mail. It started with the words: "Michael, actually many things happened here which I didn't mention. Here, I fell in love with a girl..." and continued with the secret labyrinths beneath Hagia Sophia, the things spoken by the Old Man, and new writings which had appeared in the book.

Upon returning home, Michael quickly picked up the phone with concern to call his buddy.

Nicholas was walking down the curved road near Hagia Sophia, looking with empty eyes at the old Istanbul houses. The familiarity of having being around in the area for a while was reflected in Nicholas' body language. He was going to the legendary Bosphorus Strait with visible currents, ships, and seagulls but now not necessarily for the enjoyment of its incredible beauty or to discover the city. Instead, this time it was because of the specific instruction of the Man Carrying a Water Jug who had said, "Do not drink water all day long, walk about Bosphorus, run if you wish" …

After a long walk, finally he was on the edge of the sea. The tramway near the Hagia Sophia took Nicholas to a square called Eminönü where an Ottoman mosque, the New Mosque, built several centuries ago was located. Area was humming as usual with people rushing to work. He headed to the pier. Ever since his arrival to the city, riding shuttle ferries and touring the Bosphorus strait, crossing to the opposite shore had given Nicholas a great pleasure. This one was a ferry for the vehicles on which the lower deck was for the cars and the upper was reserved for passengers. It was only a ten or fifteen minute ride to the opposite pier, but it gave an unequalled pleasure. Buying a cup of hot coffee from the ferry's canteen, sipping it while the boat gently cut through the blue strait, looking at numerous surrounding historical sites, watching the seagulls at an arm's length fighting in flight to grab the pieces of *simit* thrown by the passengers, and the magnificent sight of Hagia Sophia seen from every angle throughout the trip had almost turned into a ritual obsession for Nicholas. As the ferry lumbered away from the pier, he was looking around in joy. He bought a simit, a type of crispy warm, bagel-like, white wheat flour circular sesame covered roll dipped once quickly in dilute dark grape molasse syrup and baked according to a traditional way at large stone owens and quickly delivered to the vendors by the hundreds. With some humor unique to him, Nicholas thought of it as *The Turkish Fastfood* since anyone can grap a fresh one for a half dollar nearly at every corner of the city, in every public area. *Simit* and *Chai* pair, hot crispy roll and dark-tea combination was more popular on per capita basis than the *hamburger and cola* pair of the hinterland USA or *bagel and cream cheese* of New York. Nicholas couldn't help but see its advertising advantages. But this time around he bought neither tea nor coffee because he was instructed by the Old Man to refrain from any drinks. The simit he bought was for the daring playful seagulls already in a noisy pursuit.

The pure white seagulls were catching the simit pieces in the air and racing the ferry gliding on the deep blue chirpy waters. The combined sound of the ferries, the water and the seagulls was a relaxing symphonic therapy for his mind exhausted with questions of mysteries. As he was enjoying the *catch-it-if-you-can* contest with the seagulls, he was jerked with the phone ring. When he saw Michael's name on the screen, he said "good… finally…" and accepted the call with eyes locked on the city panorama.

Hearing Michael say, "Buddy, how goes it?" was comforting. "Good, very good. I'm feeding the seagulls, these incredible birds. How are you?"

With a concerned voice Michael said, "Well, what do you think? As good as someone who has read a mid-night e-mail piled with unbelievable things. But, let me tell you buddy, I'm happy for this situation with Kristen."

"What do you mean, middle of the night?" said Nicholas in surprise. Jokingly, " oooh buddy, you sure are in love... I've no idea what the time is there, but here it is past midnight" said Michael.

"Darn it... I forgot the time difference... Sorry about it, buddy... I thought it was your morning, too. Did I wake you up?"

"No, noo... I wasn't asleep. Your e-mail arrived just as I stepped out of the Press Lounge. But, I was worried."

"The Press Lounge?... I see, we are enjoying ourselves, aren't we?" words were followed by Nicholas' teasing laughter.

Michael not wanting to dwell on it yet, "Oh no... No such luck, buddy... It was strictly business... I'll tell you all about it later..."

"Is it the toothpaste manufacturer?"

"No, no... Something else... I'll tell you in a little while... Forget it now... Tell me what all that you've written really means... the things you've mentioned are extremely weird, I beg you buddy, wherever you're now, just head on to the airport and come back here on the first flight..."

These words were clearly indicative of Michael's worries. Nicholas, to calm down his friend, said "Take it easy for a sec, will you?"

Michael was seriously concerned, "Buddy... you are telling me you've spoken with a man who should've been dead and gone long ago... you're tellin' me you've spoken with this man in secret galleries beneath an ancient basilica...You're tellin' me that this old man is the Man Carrying a Water Jug... Dam' it, Nico... The strange book in your hand is revealing new things... and there you are feeding the seagulls and talking to me about being calm... have'u lost your frigging mind?"

Nicholas realized the severity of the situation..."just a minute, just a minute... I didn't write those to alarm you... I needed your advice... There is no visible danger anyway... I wanted to bounce it all from you... wanted to hear the sound of your logic... wanted to get your opinion on these mysterious events..."

Michael's concern was not to be calmed down with a few words. This was clearly reflected in his voice tone and sincere words.

"Buddy, if you ask me, the smart play is to grab that book and get your ass back here at once... That old man is for sure from a secret cult or somethin'... Grab the book and get back here... That book is worth piles of money...."

For a moment, Nicholas was struck cold by these words. "What are you talk'n about, what's this lots of money for the book thing?"

Michael was reluctant to talk about the Press Lounge and Ali situation. But, now that he had no choice, he had to explain it.

"Remember? I'd mentioned to you the idea of talking about the book with an art expert at the university?"

"Yes, did you?"

"Through a friend, I've linked up with someone named Alexander Keyes. A professor of antiquities ancient art... He listened carefully... said... we should rediscuss it after seeing the book... Then, the next day I received a call. From that famous auction house character, Ali Ertuğrul..."

While listening in silence, Nicholas' gaze was frozen on that small ancient Maiden's Tower in the midst of the strait. The ferry was passing by what was once a prison that witnessed a great love...

Michael, still reluctant, carried on...

"Invited me to the Press Lounge to discuss what he called an attractive offer... I had to go... Initially he offered thirty million right off the bat... A businessman acquaintance of his is apparently a Da Vinci codex collector...."

Nicholas' voice tone pitched suddenly. Angrily he said, "How could you do this? On the one hand you fear for my safety, on the other you're trying to sell a book which a strange man guided me to find it..."

Although shocked a little with this unexpected response, Michael continued softly, "noo, oh no, calm down will you, I didn't talk about selling anything... I just consulted a professor... wanted to be of some help to you... Then suddenly I got a call from a reputable person... didn't you find that book with the assistance of a priest in Jerusalem? What's that got to do with the man in Hagia Sophia?"

"What's that got to do? Micky, the Old Man had given this book blank to Da Vinci and had him write it."

"Are' u out of your mind Nicko? Buddy... Pull yourself together... Obviously you believed that man... get your head together... Da Vinci lived centuries ago... If that old man had given the book to him, his bones should have turned into dust long ago... but there he is talking to you live and kicking? How'bout that?"

The ferry had reached the opposite pier and was slowly moving in to the docks. Passengers were already rushing to the deck below. Nicholas, still angry with what he just heard, also moved while Michael continued his explanation.

"It's impossible for him to be alive today. This Man Carrying a Water Jug, alive during Jesus' time, Da Vinci's time and now in yours... What the hell is this? Is he immortal, a super hero or something?"

Still upset, Nicholas responded, "How should I know? Maybe..." This was the first time ever he had a distanced and cold attitude with Michael.

Michael, having noticed this, fairly shocked and concerned, wanted to soften the conversation: "I can't believe this, your mind's messed up, if you aren't coming over, today I'll jump on the first flight and come there."

"No... No... Stay on top of our projects. No need to come. I'll be there shortly for that big meeting anyhow... But, please don't meet or discuss anything with those people.." Nicholas' words were firm and decisive.

"OK, OK... Relax... I already told them I know nothin', I divulged no detail... What do I know anyway?"

"Then, why are they offering so much for a book they haven't seen yet?" This abrupt statement from Nicholas made it clear to Michael that something from the trusted friendship has been lost inadvertently within the last few minutes. His heart was suddenly torn apart...

Still, he made a gallant effort to put things straight, tried to salvage the situation.

"My good buddy, these men had been involved with Da Vinci for a long time... They are rich, well informed, no doubt, serious collectors... Ali is a reputable and recognized, nice gentleman... He told me that Da Vinci had been in Istanbul and Anatolia for a visit. They mentioned that he established some relationships with the Sultan of Memluks and wrote a few things during that period. Apparently he kept a diary... They are after such things... Don't worry, Ali isn't someone we should worry about too much… He is the manager of a well-known auction house… What other purpose could he possibly have?"

Nicholas was still visibly cross. His voice tone reflected his disappointment and anger. As if to cut everything short, "OK, OK… whatever… Just don't talk to them again… The book is not ours. Maybe the Man is going to ask for it"

Michael tried one more time to calm Nicholas and regain his trust, "I said alright for God's sake, didn't I? But keep this in mind… Ali said that if the Book contains other writings about water, or information about a water source, they will raise their offer to fifty million or even higher…"

There was a short silence. Nicholas disembarked from the ferry, walking fast on the promenade at the edge of water as if he had to reach a place urgently, and looking at the large cargo ships passing through.

Michael still did not comprehend fully the reasons for his buddy's reaction. He really did not have much he could add to what had been already said. While on the phone, he stepped out to his dark terrace waiting for the silence to end. He wanted Nicholas to say something positive, give a sign to set him at ease. Only the seagull sounds, ship horn blasts and the noise of traffic were heard through the receiver.

Michael wanted to end the silence and change the subject a little, "Are you gonna see him again, Nicko?"

"Of course, I am. Tonight… Tonight, I'll see him again."

This time around, it was Michael who had lost his cool.

"Nicholas, what are you chasing?"

As if having not understood what Michael had said, he repeated "what am I chasing?"

Michael continued, "Yes, what do you want? What's your purpose? Why are you after this man? Look, this business of a man in a dream, is he real, does the temple exist, has gone much beyond curiosity... Please tell me, what exactly is driving you? Where are you headed to?"

"Nothin' really, who knows... I really don't know..."

"Nothing? What do you mean... nothing?"

Nicholas was also fired up. He was stressed, frustrated far beyond Michael's assumptions. His voice rang aloud... "Just the way it is... just nothing... Don't you get it? What do you think? You think I'm doing this because I really want to? These are the results of what I had gone through as a child. We were very poor. I used to get sick all the time. Not just cold or anything... It was as if I would die. It would go on for days... injections, pills, doctors... My mother stood at my bedside all those nights. She would hide her tears from me... In those terrible nights and days I fantasized about not being sick again so that my mother wouldn't cry... but, when I woke up sick the next morning... I always thought that God did not love me... always asked my mother why God didn't love us... I shed tears while looking at the stars, questioning God... Then, at one such night, I had this dream... This dream was a hope for me. It was a sign from God... The one in my dream said, I have the secret, come and find it... Now I've found it, don't you see?.."

Once again there was a deep silence. Michael didn't know what he could say. His eyes were fixed on the night shimmer of the skyscrapers and his numb mind. Nicholas was walking fast along the shore of the Bosphorus.

Somewhat breathless, Nicholas' voice was heard clearly once again... "Please just don't talk to them again. That's all I ask of you... No need to come here... I promise, I'll be there as soon as I can..."

These decisive words were now sufficient for Michael. Just to end the conversation on good terms, he simple replied, "Don't you worry, pal... I won't be talking to nobody. You have my word."

Nicholas, also aware of the tension created, wanted to soften the air and not lose his friend, "Good buddy, I am too exhausted, too frustrated and far too confused... let me cool down a little, I'll call you very shortly".

Still worried, Michael said, "OK, I'll wait for your call. Just take it easy... This has been too rough on you... God be with you, buddy, take good care..." Hung up with mixed feelings... a little sorry that he had offended his best buddy who had been under such stress for so long... Eyes still locked on the New York night glitter, he thought he had been careless. Distant humming of the city was rising in the midst of darkness...

As soon as he entered the room, he dropped himself onto the bed. He was amazed at how quickly he made it back to the hotel. He had no strength left and was incredibly thirsty. Nicholas had travelled a lot and knew what thirst was. But never like this time… He couldn't have imagined anything like this. Tongue dried up; and throat burning… As if his lungs were afire. Each iota of his body felt the thirst. It was very hard to refrain from drinking even a drop of water. He did not have the strength to rise and turn on the room lights. In the darkness of eve, as the lit Hagia Sophia appeared magical through his window, his eyes closed in exhaustion.

In fact, his tour of the Bosphorus went well until the afternoon. This sea, separating two continents, really had a legendary beauty. After his conversation with Michael, he walked a long while along the shore of the strait looking at the ferries passing by. The medieval Maiden's Tower proudly standing in solitude like a miniature chateau in the midst of the sea appeared nearer to this side of Istanbul, the Anatolian Side. At a place called Salajak, while gazing at the Maiden's Tower, for a long while, he thought over what Michael had said. He was fairly upset with what Michael had done. But strangely, he became unable to think of anything as his eyes were glued to sea. As if he had received an expertly psychotherapy session he calmed down on the edge of water while looking at the Maiden's Tower, not only that he regained his happier mood; to his surprise, he also enjoyed it.

He took a long walk at the promenade along the shore. The surroundings were magnificent. The old Ottoman mansions lining up the shore, the sea flowing with unequalled beauty, dozens of cargo ships on the move, super luxurious yachts, tour boats, fishing vessels, and also the incredible imperial palaces on the opposite shore as well as the mansions on the other side of Istanbul...

When he reached a shoreline mosque at some walking distance from the Maiden's Tower, he took a break. This was the historical Mihrimah Sultan Mosque. Water fountains with wooden stools in front adorned the garden. He settled on a stool. Washed his face with cool fountain water. He felt comforted.

As he peeked silently to the flowing sea nearby, he mumbled: "Of course! A grail is holy only because of the person who drank from it. Why call it 'holy' if it weren't for Jesus who touched it, what significance would it have if he hadn't touched it?" He was thinking aloud. But the answer he had was not satisfying. The possibility of the cup content causing this holiness occupied his mind. What could have been in it? What could make an ordinary cup holy and bestow miracles on it? He held his face in between both hands... He didn't like asking questions without answers. Idly, he kept gazing at his environment with thoughts flowing like the strait ahead of him. Having some rest at the mosque and watching the waves on the sea rejuvenated him and gave him the energy to continue his walk. Quite a distance later, he saw the Bosphorus Bridge linking both sides of Istanbul as well as the continents of Asia and Europe. It resembled the Golden Gate Bridge. As he walked by the footing base of this giant bridge, he saw a beautifully architected old structure standing. This was the Beylerbeyi Imperial Palace. Further on the way he encountered several other Ottoman mosques. The sun heat made itself felt increasingly with each passing hour. He took advantage of the mosque fountains along the way and rested intermittently at the garden fountain kiosks called *shadirvan*.

On occasion the curving shore walk took him deeper inside land and followed a zig-zagged line. The architecture on the shores of

Bosphorus was extremely deep-rooted in high taste and had numerous examples of refined masonry as well as wood workmanship.

The tail waves displaced by the large cargo ships passing through hit the shoreline promenade wantonly. To remain dry, he avoided the occasional stronger wave by halting briefly just before it struck the walkway. It was like a catch-me-if-you-can game he played with the Bosphorus. But at an even larger one approaching, he did decide to stop as he was asking himself the question, "Why did he want me to tour the strait without drinking any water?" Tiresome questions did bother him. But, just as quickly, the sea removed the stress of it all. It was as if the city was engaged in a conversation. As if it were alive, as if it had a soul... Triggering a personal dialogue within. A strangely energizing place it was indeed...

He carried on walking. The walls of the enormous Anatolian Castle rose high on the shoreline. Nicholas hung around the castle for a long period. He touched the castle walls as he walked by. This contact was what he enjoyed most whenever he encountered an ancient structure. He felt as if he was carried back centuries to a period where he sensed the presence of those who once lived there. He had felt the same pleasant feeling in Jerusalem as he walked the Mount Olive where Jesus had also walked...

He passed by dozens of shoreline mansions with incredible variety of architectural workmanship. These were the houses of influential people of the Empire. He thought that anyone in those houses could have reached out and touched the waters of the Bosphorus. He couldn't help but wonder how pleasurable living in these places must have been. Then, there it was, the second and newer bridge of the Strait... Mehmed The Conquerer...

On the base of the bridge, he decided to take a ride to the opposite shore, and embarked a fast taxi boat. As the boat speeded across, the surrounding scenery became even more delightful. Nicholas signalled to captain the walls standing tall on the approaching shore. The captain smiled and replied, "Rumelian Castle". Sharply steered the boat in that direction. After the boat neared the shore, Nicholas jumped off right in front of the castle walls. Began walking towards Hagia Sophia. It was a long way away. He began feeling the exhaustion setting in, the heat of the sun and the thirst drying him up. He knew at that very moment that a challenge was ahead. Walking had already become a dare…

In contrast to the other shore, this side appeared to have more trees and a greener landscape. Sailboats and yachts lined up the shore. After a very long walk, he was only able to reach the other footing of the Bosphorus Bridge. He absorbed the scenery in full. He had to walk to complete the tour required of him. Thirst was pressing on. Now he did not feel as strong. His lips were already chapped with dryness.

On his way back he encountered mosques such as Ortaköy Mosque showing off unique architecture. The water fountain shadirvans looked even more inviting. He took every opportunity to refresh himself by washing his face and wetting his hair. During one such break, he remained seated longer and looked longingly at the water pouring down from a fountain. This was the first time in his life when he perceived water in a very different way. "Water… Why can't I do without you? I'd have given everything for a drop of water now…" Refreshed his face repeatedly with water. Thinking aloud again, he couldn't help but say, "It has no colour, smell, nor any distinct taste. It is so very different and peculiar …"

This substance called water was strange, indeed. He had never pondered on water so deeply. Actually, he hadn't really thought of it at all. He had drunk, showered with it and watered his plants. But he hadn't stopped to think about this colorless liquid. As he observed the fountain water, he pondered his thirst and bewildering desire for water asking himself, 'what is this stuff called water?' It was yet another question without an answer. Departed the mosque shadirvan and paced himself further towards Hagia Sophia.

What had caught his eye was the outstanding architecture of the Çırağan Palace seen little ahead. By the time he reached it, he was already very tired and did not have the strength to visit it. Futher down the road, he met with the famous Dolmabahçe, yet another imperial palace on the coastline. The quality of masonry workmanship was evident even in the remotest corners of the structure. Its garden pools were drawing Nicholas nearer. It was now much harder for him to resist the temptation of drinking some water and he was struggling with the idea. All the while, instructions given by the Old Man were on his mind. Although he had initially thought of the grail as holy "obviously because of who had drank from it", now, all three possibilites appeared logical. But he thought, "since he asked, only one must be the correct answer". As he gazed at the sea, he reconsidered that it must be due to the person who drank from it and thinking aloud again, he said "otherwise, what difference would it have from a regular cup that I use, for instance?" He had finally reached his limits. Each cell in his body burnt with the thirst.

The dark was settling on the city and the magical glamour of lights began enveloping it. At long last, he made it as far as the old Galata Bridge spanning the Golden Horn. Hundreds of people were lined up with their fishing poles at the railings of the crowded bridge. Dragging himself through, Nicholas had the sight of Hagia Sophia ahead of him. He made one last gallant effort to reach his hotel at once. Soon the tour would be over just as he was told. Without a drop of water, without a morsel to eat...

When he opened his eyes, he realized that he was awakened in a different mood. Occasional distant horns of vehicles in the nearby traffic were being heard in the city which did not appear to sleep at all. Reminded him of New York… He remained motionless with eyes open in the darkness hued only with the gentle light of the city glitter. He felt no desire to move. His legs were still hurting. Deepened thirst was everywhere. The bedside digital clock showed 02:27 AM in large mildly lit figures. Thinking he was twins with this number 27, he tried to ignore it. After all that he had been through, he was at a point where he was certain that it meant something, but prayed and hoped no evil would come from it.

Finally he was able to pull himself together. Stepped into shower. This did help, but thirst was as persistent as ever. This was the first time in his life he experienced fasting. He knew that shortly this will all be over. Smiling for a brief moment with eyes closed under the rushing shower water, he thought of it as part of a commando training. But he knew instinctively that if he hadn't collapsed and slept before, he couldn't have endured thirst for so long. Too much activity on foot was not the right thing to do. He realized that he could have kept his promise to the Old Man more wisely and still remained a little stronger. As if to justify his choices in a sunny, breezy day afoot far too long, but somewhat jubilant under the shower, "Niko Ma'boy!.. This is Istanbul... not some second rate shit hole...", he thought, "...how can you stay in one place longer than a brief stop... If Kristen was here I could have sat with her all day long at a cool joint with a view of the ancient world... that would have been nice... anyway, the Old Man said... do not drink or eat... so here it is I've done it... kept my word... would he have known if I hadn't... no, I couldn't have cheated him... I like him... there must be some secret attached to this... we shall see what fate has in store for us..." Shower did help. He was almost his old self again... But, still painfully thirsty...

He stepped out to his small balcony. Witness to centuries gone by and still standing in solitude, the bright Hagia Sophia was as mysterious as ever at night. Very aware of the unique connection he shared with the basilica, Nicholas stayed fairly calm and motionless for a long while on the balcony viewing the panorama of the busy night pregnant to events yet to come... He did wonder what Kristen had been doing since her departure. During the day trip he had frequently thought of dropping a message to Kristen, but hesitated. Flight to New York would have taken at least around 10-11 hours. After being on the phone with Michael, while trying to calm down his anger, he was reminded of the New York time and thought with anguish that his "Kristen must have already arrived home". He was already longing for her beyond his comprehension. Thoughts of chasing after her to the fire of happiness and jumping into the arms of love had crossed his mind several times. He wanted to hear her voice, but didn't risk it thinking he might be misunderstood. He was in love. He felt they reached out to each other in a sincere way. He could have taken the risk to ask, at least, how the trip had gone. But he couldn't. She was a breathtakingly, mesmerizingly beautiful woman, the thought of losing her was terrifying. Especially after what this Old Man, the One Carrying a Water Jug, had said about women, he looked at Kristen from a very different angle. Just Kristen? No, he viewed every woman differently. When he focused and considered women thoughtfully, he realized how right the Old Man was. Truly, each woman possessed a unique beauty. He did want to admit that "God creates each with great and special care". Not only to women seen around, but he also felt changes in his attitude toward his own mother. He did not neglect calling her nearly every morning and entertaining her with jokes after saying, "Hi, mommy..." first. She kept responding, "What happened to you in Istanbul, did a magical wand strike you, son?.. Oh, whatever it is... Thank you my darling... I'm so happy to hear from you so frequently... Do keep it up, son!" His change of attitude also pleased Nicholas. But when the topic was Kristen, he could not recognize himself... A man who could easily and impressively speak at business meetings was unable to utter a word in the presence of this sweet girl and was tongue bound. It didn't make any sense, but it was what it was. Perhaps, love did change people after all!

He stepped back into his room. He wanted time to elapse faster and meet the Old Man at once. He still felt a little tired, but his thirst had reached the final limits. He thought to occupy himself a little on Facebook. The very moment the page appeared on his screen, messages and connection requests popped up on the screen. He glimpsed at them from a distance without acknowledging any but Kristen's name in the list, which suddenly elated him. His heart pumping fast, he opened her message right away...

"Hiii... Howdy? In NY already... Had a good time with you... Thx for everything. Wish I'd have stayed longer. Istanbul is on my mind. Call me when you get back!"

He jumped up in joy. In a moment, there was no trace of anything, no thirst, no pain in the legs, no tiredness. All gone... A few words from the loved one erased everything. He immediately wrote a reply, desperately wanting to finish it saying, "I love you".

With happiness, and like a mischievous child, he thought for a few moments, then satisfied with his idea, published a short note hinting at Kristen:

"With deepest feelings to the One:

Alas... Heart in love, has fallen apart cross with the words silent,

Wondering why such cruelty, fears of emotion, befallen dissent!

Roared the hushed tongue. Why such adoration Oh Crazed Heart?

Could I've done more? With feelings exceeding my meager talent!"

For a while he looked at Kristen's photos at her Facebook page. She had already uploaded the Istanbul pictures including those taken with Nicholas. Amber and Kristen had written sweet comments and already many of their friends responded with pleasant statements. Amber's comment referring to Nicholas on their jointly taken photos saying, "our very special friend" and Kristen's emoticon of a small heart made him walk on air. He was, an adult, jumping up and down in his hotel room at this strange hour of the night. But he did not care... At that moment the alarm clock in his mobile signaled that the time was 03:10 AM. He had taken the precaution of setting the alarm before going to sleep in his exhausted and dehydrated body. That strange excitement and fear enveloped him suddenly and totally removed the Kristen jubilation. He turned off his computer. Quickly dressed. Left the hotel in a rush.

Once again the summer night outside was pleasant and fairly quiet. He walked fast without paying much attention to his surroundings. Within a few minutes he was in front of the Hagia Sophia garden gate. It was 03:24 AM!

It did appear as if no one was in the garden. Waited. Now, he had no sense of thirst. For a moment felt himself trembling. The questions unanswered were once again churning in his mind. His body felt tense. He saw a silhouette approaching in the dark. Looked at his watch: 03:27 exactly.

It was the same attendant who had previously accompanied him to the Man Carrying a Water Jug. It was clear that this man was Old Man's assistant or servant.

"Welcome, Mr. Nicholas", and he gently opened the gate. Nicholas responded respectfully, "Thank you!" Without any additional words, he silently followed the attendant as usual to the main entrance of the temple. The main entrance door did not open easily. He welcomed Nicholas in with a polite reverence. The doors shut noisily behind Nicholas. Once again the Man Carrying a Water Jug and Nicholas were the only ones inside.

The Man Carrying a Water Jug was sitting at the central point beneath the dome, the spot he knew so well from his dreams. Nicholas walked respectfully towards the center.

The Old Man had crimson cloth in front of him spread on the floor. This spread had a glass and a bottle which appeared to contain water. Judging from the mist on the bottle, he concluded that it was cold. A plate on the cloth had some of that *tahini* sweet *halva,* and several slices of bread. The man smiled and said, "Welcome Nicholas. How was your day?" Nicholas replied: "It was fine, Sir". He couldn't have possibly complained about the tiring day and his extreme thirst. The Old Man gestured at him to take a seat and continued: "Please sit. You must be tired."

When Nicholas took a seat at the edge of the cloth, the Old Man began talking in his usual pleasant manner. "Well, how are you? Are you thirsty?"

If this question was posed to him by a friend or acquaintance, his quick response would have easily been "…are you f'n kiddin'me, I'm about to croak from thirst", but he behaved himself and was able to gently say, "Yes… Sir. I'm very very thirsty…"

The Old Man took a deep sighing breath and spoke in a serious tone:

"Living beings need water. This is a biological reality. Living beings thirst and desire water. Earth itself, life on it and in it needs water. Dehydration has been explained in terms of biology… But why and how do we *feel* thirst? This is a big mystery."

Silence hung in the air for a while at the end of his words. The question posed was profound. "How do we really 'feel' our thirst? What is the mechanism?" were the secondary questions which raced through Nicholas' mind. As Nicholas was further contemplating the words said, in expectation of revelations, he was also looking at the Old Man, and wondering the "big mystery". The Sage was silent, he simply filled the glass and extended it to Nicholas with a not so steady hand. He added commandingly, "Sip it very slowly! Take only minute droplets. Swallow not in haste, and listen to me very intently".

Nicholas could have swallowed the whole bottle in one gulp. He simply surrendered politely in his obedient way, "Yes, Sir…" Just as he aimed for the first little drop of the long day, he was jolted with the affectionate but warning question of the Old Man:

"My young friend, what are you doing? That is no way to drink water. You should never drink water with your eyes open. If you want to absorb the full strength of water, if you desire a long, healthy and peaceful life, you must close your eyes and concentrate. Take a little sip, wait, swallow, wait again and then open your eyes and breathe before the next sip. Always drink water in this way and always be seated. This is the only way by which you can receive its power."

Nicholas, without any reply, did as he was told. The pleasure he received was surreal. He did not care whether it was his immense thirst or the different taste causing this pleasure. The Old Man continued:

"A believer is between the Creator and Jesus. Between God and a human is WATER. Never forget these words. You will never hear this secret from someone else. This is the greatest and most important of all secrets."

Eyes firmly closed, and in accompaniment of these mystical words, Nicholas took small sips in the proper sequence and tried to quench his thirst which had climaxed with the first taste. Nothing could be more beautiful. He did not understand why the eyes had to be shut but it did not matter, it was an incredible joy. The pleasant voice of the Old Man was echoing gently and softly in Hagia Sophia.

"Nicholas," he said, "do you now comprehend why I wanted you to spend a full day without a drop of water?"

Nicholas swallowed, took a breath, opened his eyes and replied, "I had some ideas, but I failed to fully understand it".

The nice smile of his host had fully spread and glittering in his old tired eyes which must have witnessed so much in long times gone by.

"Listen well... Let me tell you the reasons."

"Think of the places where Jesus lived. You were there. You saw... We beckoned you there just as we had called Leonardo, Nostradamus, Newton and others... all in their own good time...

We did not call you so that you may dig and find a book. We wanted you to see the lands, the soil, rock and stones where he lived... Of course in those days, unlike today, those lands were more arid and lacked water. David, Solomon, Abraham lived in such places. Almost a desert everywhere... Sun baked places... Thorns, some dates, goats and a few camels... Created by God for such conditions... All capable of resisting heat and thirst... Man's creation secrets are hidden in those places... No one ever considers why God saw fit for Jesus to live in such troublesome places... Why not in places where lands were like paradise with waters, oceans, forests, and rivers? For an invaluable being like Jesus? Why?"

Nicholas kept to his drinking regime as he listened intently and in great curiosity. The few seconds which had just elapsed, the silent interval of the Old Man seemed like an age to Nicholas as he awaited anxiously.

"God's choice of such unforgiving places is one of his magnificent secrets. God enabled Jesus' life in those places... The reason for this is the secret of creation on Earth. Water was extremely scarce there. If you were to know what *Water* is, you would have also understood why God chose that place for Jesus..."

Nicholas was awed with what he was hearing. The Old Man picked up the bottle and poured a little more precious water to Nicholas' glass.

"Mankind does not appreciate the value of abundance, what he does not lack... He does not take protect of it and does not pay the required attention... He only comprehends its value after losing it... Jesus was bestowed to those places because water, God's most magical creation, was most scarce and people would have been more inclined to grasp the miracles. Teachings would have been easier to convey to those who knew suffering and appreciated the value of a drop of life. This is why Jesus had to live among those people, in desert like places...

I wanted you to walk about without a drop of water all day because this was the only way for you to greatly appreciate a cup of water. So that you may look at life in the same way you looked at a drop of water while in great thirst. So that you may consider water with much greater respect and realize its divine magnificence."

The echo in the basilica continued for an extra brief moment or two when the Old Man finished his words. They also resonated in Nicholas' mind. He had never thought of this before. True... Jesus lived in such harsh places... not in paradise on earth... His host continued:

"Recall the conversation Jesus had with the Samaritan woman. Jesus had said for the well water at her house, 'anyone who drinks this will thirst again, but those who drink mine will be quenched for eternity. The water I give shall be the spring of eternal life.' The well water of the Samaritan was what we all drink. Which water of eternal life did Jesus refer to? This is mentioned in the Bible, but no one ever considers the 'WATER' mentioned by Jesus. Jesus revealed the greatest secret there. It was as if he was screaming there the real secret of immortality.

The Bible contains so much mysterious information that it is beyond your imaginations. A sentence, a word within the stories contains incredible mysteries... We showed some of those to Isaac Newton."

Nicholas was intoxicated. He was lost somewhere between the wisdom conveyed and delicious drops of water drunk with eyes closed. He was speechless.

Affectionately, the Old Man said, "you may let go of water and eat some of this sweet". He put some of the cubic *tahini* sweets in flat bread and offered it to Nicholas. The thought of "sweet in a slice of bread?" seemed peculiar to him, but he accepted it in humility with gratitude. He wasn't very hungry. The sips of water seemed to have suppressed his hunger which was not overwhelming to begin with. Thirst was a more pressing day-long problem. He took a bite from the sweet sandwiched in flat bread. It was delicious. This delicacy called *tahini halva* was referred to as a sort of dessert, but in fact it was something totally different. It wasn't too sweet to begin with, and made one feel full even with the first bite. As Nicholas enjoyed his snack and chased it with occasional sips of water, the Old Man spoke with a more lowered voice.

"Rain drops, dew on leaves, water dripping from a tap, drops from pointy icicles hanging from leaves... drops one at a time... one by one... pearl like tears from beautiful eyes....
Observe! Listen to their sounds... if you can listen... if you can hear...

Think of the first rain droplets striking your face... Floods may gather from these... If earth welcomes it, abundance of blossom ensues... If not, a disaster may prevail... God's power and strength is concealed in that one little droplet..."

Nicholas was mesmerized with these wise words rooted in ancient knowledge and wisdom, leading to endless implications... The mild echo of the Old Man's low voice still lingered in the basilica main hall, adding totally unfamiliar dimensions of realization to Nicholas' mental intoxication.

"Water has a harmony which cannot be described. It has a color but cannot be categorized in the spectrum. It has an aroma, but nobody knows how to explain it... other than sweet, pleasant, comforting and divine... It has a taste, but can you tell me what it is other than satisfying, nice, cool and quenching... Did you ever think about these Nicholas?"

Nicholas lowered his head in admission of ignorance. As the Old Man slowly rose from his seat with the aged and tired motions, he comforted his young friend saying, "Do not fret, do not be saddened... No human being ever seriously ponders this... an odd one perhaps... may be one in a million if you are lucky... "

Just as Nicholas was attempting to stand, the Old Man was already up like an ancient monument with eyes fixated at the dome. His gaze to the heavens was thoughtful and appeared sad... His silent and tired face seemed to have the worries of One engaged in deep reflection... For a moment he appeared to have travelled through many millennia and many dimensions... Seemed he had gone billions of miles in search of the truth... Eyes still at the dome, he spoke like a loving and patient elder, a teacher:

"There is no other substance purer, softer, more peaceful, obedient and gentler than water... None conforms so ideally and with subtlety, none has a superior power against hardness... None cleanses better the soul and body... Just like air, no other is so essential... A microscopic droplet freezing in a infinitesimal cavity can crack a gigantic rock. Can move a ship in the form of steam. Mankind does not conform to water as it does to humans and other beings... No other creature than man harms water intentionally... None commits a greater sin..."

Then, as if he had forgiven all the sins he had witnessed, he turned and smiled, put his hand on Nicholas, "Come, let's walk and chat a little."

Nicholas was quick to reply with pleasure, "Of course, Sir." He stepped forward keeping a very close but respectful distance to the Old Man. He didn't want to miss a single uttered word... The gentle sounds of even soft walking steps of the duodid amplify beneath the dome...

"Water existed before the planets, earth, the sun and the moon. Not even the stars were born yet... Not the galaxy... No light anywhere... There was only Water. God's first creation is WATER... And loved it... Bestowed on it magnificent powers and passed it on... All the rest of creation was derived from it... The 'rest' means all visible and invisible life forms... the living and the non-living... Water is in everything... What does this all mean?"

A few moments of silence followed... They were walking again up the curved path to the upper floor. Nicholas did not know if he should reply in any manner, but preferred to remain silent.

"What God has said with Water is: *I am in everything... My power is in everything...*"

They reached the upper floor. The Old Man opened a door on the side with a key from his purse pocket. Small steps climbing were ahead. Nicholas behind, the Sage in front, they climbed up slowly. His words in the narrow upward corridor were now much stronger:

"In all that is manifested and evident, the essence, the secret, power and strength are what remain in the invisible. These words contain the key to God's heavenly secrets. Think on these words well… Find the secrets…"

He stopped on the steps. He was tired. His breathing suggested that a brief stop was necessary. He turned back and in the twilight of darkness looked piercingly into Nicholas' eyes…

"Look at what our Lord Jesus says from centuries ago: Those who seek should not cease till they find that which is sought, and they shall be glad upon finding it, and pleased, they shall rule over all that is."

After a short break, they continued up the stairs. A few steps later the Old Man stopped. There was a door ahead. He opened it. The moment they stepped out, the scenery which welcomed them was incredible. The night sky, stars above and the Bosphorus below...

They were on the side of the main dome at the very top of Hagia Sophia. The spot they were on was very high. Hagia Sophia was already on a hill and when its own height was added to that, it provided an amazing Istanbul panorama. The Bosphorus was flowing with all its beauty and the bridges over it, the Maiden's Tower and the palaces were easy to pick. Ottoman Empire had furbished this mystical capital with numerous mosques. This massive city was built on seven hills and nearly all of them were crowned with a magnificent Ottoman mosque. Nicholas, at the top of Hagia Sophia, was now looking at the scenery in admiration.

The Man Carrying a Water Jug began walking slowly on the narrow edge with the jug in one hand and the other touching the dome. As the Old Man walked gently around the dome, Nicholas was close behind him with eyes locked on the view. The short silence was interrupted with the man's slightly harsh voice:

"God made water a catalyst for each of his creations. After diluting his unimaginable power in water to a tolerable level, he created everything in a planned and measured way. He hid all secrets in Water. On it he did not bestow a color, an aroma, a describable taste but he hid all of these in the water. Thus the mystery of water… God did not reveal to anyone why he created the water, not even to Jesus. Why did He create water? Why create everything from water? This is a secret. He created earth to make water visible. The very first creation is water. Water revolves endlessly from one state to another as vapor, rain, snow, ice and back to water again. We observe these as physical events and accept it as the way of nature. But why is it so? This is a secret hidden in the holy books."

Nicholas was hypnotized and speechless. The Old Man stopped suddenly. They were on the Topkapi Palace side of the dome. The wise old man carefully placed the jug down and slowly sat down and signaled to Nicholas to do the same. Nicholas sat next to him. They both had their feet dangling at the roof top. They both took in the scene silently. Nicholas' mind was preoccupied with the incredible words he had just heard.

The Old Man suddenly turned to Nicholas and asked: "Do you smell it?"

Nicholas, surprised with the question, tried to sense the aroma in the air. There seemed to be a small touch of pleasant food aroma.

"Oh, yes, it smells like delicious fish on grills".

The Old Man pointed at the Galata Bridge and said, "The aroma is from the fish restaurants below the bridge. Not too far from here… There you feel the aroma right in your body. It is not like a smell just a little away or near. Pay attention, and you will feel it right inside you…"

It was yet another seemingly mysterious statement from the Old Man. Nicholas pondered a little. Then he tried to smell the air more carefully. He thought it strange that he couldn't place its source anywhere. It was as if the aroma was inside him. It was unusual.

The Old Man smiled and looked at Nicholas.

"Let me give you a secret that will change you and your life. Listen carefully and be aware. Eye is simply an instrument which processes light rays. We see. But it is not clear how… We see the object where it is and not inside us or in our head…" Pointing at the Galata Bridge, he said "Look, you are seeing the bridge exactly where it is, at its correct location".

Nicholas nodded like an obedient student confirming his comprehension.

"Ear is an instrument… We hear but how? This is not clear… We always hear the sound at its original source, not in our ear or heads…" Again he pointed at the bridge and said "you are hearing distant car noises on the bridge… you hear them right on the bridge, nowhere else… right on the bridge.."

Nicholas simply said, "Yes, Sir" as if wanting to validate.

The Old Man carried on with slow distinct words.

"Nose is an instrument. We smell… Inside us… Not outside like eyes and ears, not where it is. Aroma is inside us…"

Silence took over again. The Old Man uttered mystical sentences and turned his gaze to the view ahead. Nicholas tried to comprehend. It was true... This simple truth he hadn't noticed before. While the bridge and noise was there the grilled fish aroma was within. Inside him...

The Old Man turned his eyes slowly back at Nicholas and added:

"Try to solve this small mystery... If you can solve this, then boundaries of your mind will expand, the curtains will rise... Why do we smell through our noses and feel it inside? Why can't we say it is distant like the bridge and sounds? Naturally at this moment, like all other humans, you are using less than 10% of your mind... If you can solve this, all obstacles and limits to your mind will be removed..."

He tapped Nicholas' shoulder affectionately. Then with a sweet smile he continued:

"Those who seek should not abandon what they seek until they find it. Upon finding it he will be surprised and in his surprise he shall admire and rule over all things. Solve the mystery and rule over all things..."

A thick silence followed... The Sage was now looking back at the Bosphorus. Nicholas did the same in mixed feelings, but couldn't help but catch a glimpse or two of the Old Man. Who was this man? What was he trying to do? It was impossible to grasp the mysterious essence of what was being said.

He wanted to reply saying, "You have called both Da Vinci and Isaac Newton, just as you've called me. OK, but who are you really?" But he couldn't... As he was submerged in these thoughts, he was startled with the Old Man's voice.

"There is something you want to say, go on, what is it? Say it".

Nicholas was shocked. He remembered the warning of Da Vinci... No questions... Otherwise the journey will end... He still wanted to know how someone from ages past could still be alive. Stayed silent for a moment or two, but couldn't resist the temptation. Especially after his conversation with Michael earlier, he had to get it out of his chest.

He simply uttered, "I apologize, Sir...but..."

"...My best friend and partner Michael has been very concerned all along during my trip to Jerusalem and here... That book I found in Jerusalem before meeting you... well... he apparently asked about this book to a university professor. He apparently divulged some information about the book and its content... He mentioned Da Vinci as the author... But, he also had said that the book was purchased from an old bookstore in Istanbul... Then some auctioneer contacted him and they apparently spoke about the book. Believe me I had no knowledge... If I had known, I would have never permitted it... These men offered a very serious amount of money for the book. Please don't get me wrong... I'll not do such a thing... I really apologize, but I thought you should know about it... I told Michael to stay away from those people... He won't speak to them again, ever..."

Nicholas was feeling very guilty and lowered his head in shame.

The Man Carrying a Water Jug raised his eyes from the Bosphorus to the night sky... Spoke gently as he gazed the stars...

"Humans never change... Men today are trying to do the same what Alexander III of Macedon and Genghis Khan tried with their rule and armies... This time only with money... That insane desire is still conquering the souls of men...."

Nicholas was perplexed. The Sage noticed this and said, "you didn't understand, did you?" Nicholas admitted, "I'm sorry... I didn't understand..." His gaze moving back to the night sky, the Old Man proceeded to explain:

"Alexander and Genghis were powerful rulers. The two men lived in different centuries. They had great armies. Everyone thinks that these two men were in the pursuit of ruling the world. Their conquests had already reached far and beyond... One could traverse their lands on horseback with a journey which will last a very long time. Their rule seemed boundless... But they kept on moving... kept on fighting... kept on conquest after conquest... This is the reason why today's people think that these men were after a World rule... They already had acquired unimaginable power, tasted all pleasures of the world. One cannot imagine the pleasures they enjoyed... They wanted this to never end... They even desired to be immortal... to conquer death... But they were not really after ruling the world... They just wanted to be rulers forever and their pleasures to never end... Until eternity..."

Nicholas joined in without being too aggressive.

"Is it not an impossible demand? Why would people who have achieved so much ask for something impossible?"

The Old Man smiled in a sorrow audible in his words.

"If you have a life of great pleasure, then you would do almost anything to maintain it. Do not forget these men were powerful rulers and commanders. The pleasures they had in life is beyond anyone's imagination. It is incomprehensible... One could only describe it as a dream... By the way, I too was a great ruler and commander once..."

Nicholas was absolutely shocked by his last words. He was frozen stiff with his eyes on the Sage. Now he was definitely, totally and absolutely confused in the midst of a whirlwind emotional storm. His mind was about to explode... Who was this man? Did he not say that he was the Man Carrying a Water Jug whom the Bible mentions? Nicholas was absorbed in the words, "...I too was a great ruler and commander..." Nothing seemed to make any sense any more... The Old Man was still talking:

"Sages had given them the only way to fulfill their desires. This is why their lives were spent in an endless pursuit, on a path with no end... The sages had spoken of a water spring somewhere in the World... A spring from the same source but which flowed from two far apart places... These men were not enlarging their conquests... They were searching for that water... The elixir of immortality..."

Nicholas couldn't help repeating, "the water of immortality?"

"Yes, the water of immortality... the water of life..." said the Old Man and stood up. Nicholas followed suit while repeating "water of immortality?" He was following the Sage closely hoping to hear a few more explanations. But the Old Man kept walking... They completed the circle around the dome and walked back through the same door. The Old Man in front, Nicholas right behind, they walked down slowly on the narrow stairs... They reached the second floor of Hagia Sophia. The Old Man locked the door and headed toward the spiral ramp and began talking again in the narrow curved tunnel which would take them to the ground level of the Basilica.

"Water... God transposes power through it... Everything is created from water... Water also is created by God. And, this is easy for God... Understanding water is very difficult...

Those who learn the real meaning of water will eventually resolve the mysteries. If you read the holy books carefully, you will see that these mysteries are scattered generously in them."

The Old Man became silent again. When they reached the ground floor, he headed to the main gate to the Hagia Sophia garden. Nicholas followed him as usual. When they reached the fountain kiosk, the Old Man who clearly was a Sage himself, turned on the water tap. As he was observing the water flow, he spoke again with his misty voice:

"Water... sparkles of light in it... glimmer of life moves inside it... Silence is hidden in it... Pure warmth, desolate loneliness, silent safety... Think much on these words... These are not empty utterances... A secret from thousands of years... I wish to give you a secret through these words but you must find it".

Nicholas, while standing behind him and looking at the same water, kept repeating the words in astonishment and with a pounding heart wanting to memorize:

"Water... sparkles of light in it... glimmer of life moves there... Silence is hidden in it... Pure warmth, desolate loneliness, silent safety..."

After sprinkling his face with water, the Sage stood smiling... In the meantime, Nicholas was far too disturbed with the thought of appearing like a treasure hunter wanting to sell Da Vinci's "Book of Secrets" which the Old Man had guided him to find. He was really ashamed of this situation in which he had no intentional role. Although he had honestly explained it, the Old Man's silence on the subject multiplied Nicholas' shame. Nicholas, encouraged by Old Man's smile, said:

"I hope... Sir... you are not annoyed with me... I really didn't know anything about what happened in New York concerning the book. My friend had just spoken briefly about the book to a professor... We never had any intentions of selling it... I apologize... really... I apologize..."

The Sage bent down without saying a word and took the water jug which he never left away from his sight... Began walking toward the small garden behind the Basilica. His silence multiplied Nicholas' worries... His fear was partly responsible for his statement... He was afraid to lose the 'journey' and see it 'end' as he had been warned. Especially now when nothing had been clearly resolved... He was following the Sage with this fear in his heart.

Just as he uttered the words, "I really am sorry" wanting to reinforce his innocence, the Old Man interrupted him:

"This morning you will return to America at once... You no longer can stay here..."

Nicholas was shocked. It was as if he was in flames within. Was Da Vinci's warning becoming a reality? Was the Journey ending without ever beginning, without understanding anything, with all the mysteries and secrets? In response to this unexpected shock, he blurted "but, Sir, why?"

Then he pulled himself together recalling the caution of not asking questions... Just as Nicholas continued, "I am sorry, Sir, of course, I'll return immediately... I wish I could've stayed with you longer... There are so many unanswered questions..." he was interrupted again:

"If your friend uttered the words 'Da Vinci','Istanbul','Water', 'Mona Lisa', 'Moon' and 'Book' together, then you can't imagine how dangerous and sinister those men could be. I forbade Da Vinci to reveal any secrets and he placed them in his paintings. I forbade Michel de Nostradamus to describe what he had seen during our travel between universes, this is why his writings appear so strange… Those men after the Book will do everything in their power. Under any circumstances, do not meet those men. Let your friend handle it… You must sell the book… Otherwise they will never leave you alone and you might be murdered…"

With these words, Nicholas' existing concerns were suddenly transformed into terror. Extremely worried, he confirmed his acceptance by saying "Of course, we'll do exactly as you command…" And, added: "But I'll be seeing you, won't I? Please say yes…" His words clearly reflected the sorrow he was feeling. The Sage walking fairly rapidly ahead of him turned back suddenly, pierced at Nicholas and said:

"I did not tell you that the Journey had ended… I told you that now you must go… We shall meet again after we get over this critical situation you are in…"

Smiling, he stepped forward to the rear garden. Nicholas was very comforted. He was happy to hear that the Journey was not at an end. But this joy did not last more than a few moments… His buddy Michael who was worried about Nicholas meeting a strange man in Istanbul was now in real danger in New York. Could he be in danger at this very moment? Nicholas was now thrown into a new darkness where he did not want to think of any dark possibilities.

They were now in the back garden of Hagia Sophia. There was a wooden table and few chairs. The Sage took a seat. Gestured at Nicholas to take the opposing chair. As Nicholas carefully joined him, the Old Man began talking, "Don't worry. Nothing to fear… Tell your friend to bargain very hard… Let him raise the price much higher... Let him sell. But, make sure you sell it... Do you understand?"

Nicholas nodded very distinctly to indicate his full comprehension of the instructions just received. Now he was a little more at ease. But his concerns were overwhelming him. Just to reassure himself and alleviate his fears, he asked: "You said murder... If my friend sells the book nothing will happen, right? There won't be any problems?" In trepidation he was looking at Old Man's eyes.

"Sell... and never contact them again... Nothing will happen. Do not worry. God will protect you..."

Carried on looking into Nicholas' worried eyes:

"When you are sowing your field or harvesting... Prior to picking fruits, making bread, cooking, drinking water, playing ball, reading, writing, driving, riding an aircraft, stepping out of your home, going to church, but especially in rainy and thunderous days, make sure your whole body is thoroughly washed with water. Even under the direst conditions you must wash your whole body once at least every two days... If you do all I have said until now and what I'll be telling you from now on... God will be with you... God's power will stand with you..."

Nicholas immediately confirmed, saying that he would follow the instructions thoroughly. Just as he said it, he caught a glimpse of a figure approaching them. This was the attendant who always welcomed him to Hagia Sophia. The attendant silently and respectfully placed two tea cups on the table and pulled back in reverence.

The Sage took a sip and looked at Nicholas as he spoke, "At the dome when I asked you what was bothering you, I knew that you had many questions… You still do… But as I told you previously this is not a Journey of question and answer between you and me. So far it progressed as it should. Just as with those who were chosen before you, as they were informed… Yet I ask you once again. What is your real question? The most essential question? Ask me what really has been gnawing your mind… I may not allow another chance like this…"

Nicholas was quite mixed up. The dreams which had been repeating for years brought him here. What was this whirlwind storms eye in which he now found himself? This was beyond his comprehension. His mind was on fire with the desire to understand all that happened until that very moment… For a second he hesitated, but the encouraging gaze of the Sage encouraged him and in his most respectful manner he looked at the Old Man:

"Sir, I am speechless. What I have heard from you to this second astonished me and I'm enchanted. When you permitted a question at the dome, I was under the cloud of doubts… I didn't know how to phrase my questions in fear of offending you… Please do not misunderstand my words… But, up at the dome, I was about to ask you the Man Carrying a Water Jug mentioned in the Bible, the person described by our Lord Jesus in Jerusalem, if that person is you, how could you be alive in this century, I was about to say this is impossible… But, this elixir of immortality you've mentioned is confusing me. Please tell me who you are…"

When Nicholas finished his words it was as if the weight of the planet was lifted off his shoulders. At long last, he managed to ask the most perplexing question on his mind. Now he was awaiting the response worriedly.

The Sage leaned toward the table. Spoke softly and slowly:

"I am the Man Carrying a Water Jug". We are free of falsehood. Let this be a lesson to you. Always remain free of lies and falsehood. I understand you well. Like the most you, too, are biased and have doubts like most because of the wrong assumptions accepted as truths. You fail to understand... have suspicions. I have always given three question chances to those chosen. I have given you your chances also. Do not ever forget this... No more questions... Otherwise the Journey will end... Listen well because we are about to do something which is more difficult than splitting an atom. We shall destroy your biases."

Nicholas was in pure attention and fear... The destruction of biases and preconceptions. He was all ears as the Man Carrying a Water Jug continued to speak softly.

"What people call 'time' is a most curious phenomenon, is it not? Recall your childhood... Time did not seem to move forward. Days would never pass. Is this not true without any exception in childhood of every living soul? But when you are older, time moves so fast. Then, you look back and express those times which seemed to move so slowly in years, in decades... Days, months, years chase one another... Then, time is no longer sufficient for all the things you wish to be able to do. What then makes the elder feel the rapid passage of time which once moved so slowly?"

The Old Man picked his tea glass as if in slow motion. Took a sip. Observed his surroundings as if he was at a different dimension. He was revealing the essence of many mysteries in the garden of this most fantastic temple which itself seemed to defy time... Now a little firm and sharp, the Man Carrying a Water Jug from the Bible simply said with his unique voice as if arising from the ages past:

"In fact, there is no such thing as *time*"

"When you consider it, you will see that there is no such thing as *time*. Not in the sense currently thought or accepted. Time does not elapse… in reality what passes is you… now the most anyone can say is that the time flows like water..."

Nicholas was speechless. He was listening in astonishment, trying to comprehend. The Old Man was observing the sky while sipping his tea. A few moments later, the Sage placed the empty glass on the table and picked up from where he left:

"If you were to place a reflector at a suitable spot in space and look at it with a telescope on Earth, you could see the landing of Apollo and watch live the first step taken on the Moon by Neil Armstrong. Did you know it? All scientists working for NASA know this."

Nicholas did not utter a word or want to ask a question. He had already used his share of allowed questions. But this amazing statement was out of this world. How could anyone watch live on a reflector what took place in July 1969?

The Old Man, as if he had read the mind of Nicholas, smiled and explained, "If you were to place a reflector at a location 40 light years ahead of the Moon, then you could watch the same live broadcast of 1969 watched by 33 million people of the yester world. Watch Neil Armstrong take his first personally small, but universally giant step of humanity on the Moon."

Nicholas was familiar with certain laws of physics, but he hadn't ever thought of these subjects in this manner. He was aware that he had to let go of the war between his conceptions assumed correct and what he was hearing from the wise Sage. He felt that the time arrived for a radical change.

The Old Man looked up at the starry night sky and said, "Look at the sky Nicholas". He obeyed and looked at the night sky above Hagia Sophia.

"Nicholas, are you aware that the glimmer of light we see this very moment departed from the stars and galaxies many many ages ago... the light which had left the stars immense periods ago have traversed the universe and reached us at this very moment... So incredibly distant, so far away…. they have just arrived..."

Nicholas, hesitantly, turned his eyes to the Old Man who was still fixed on the stars. Nicholas softly responded:

"I enjoy documentaries on the Cosmos. I've learned that the light of the nearest star reaches us in 4.5 years of our time…"

He was looking reservedly at the Old Man. As if eyes fixed at eternity, the wise Sage facing the night sky softly took over from where Nicholas left:

"Correct… That's the nearest one which your astronomers call Alpha Centauri. 4.5 years exactly…"

Then he lifted up his right arm pointing at a spot at the night sky. Nicholas tried to focus his tired eyes at that spot.

"There it is. The Alpha Centauri… that tiny glitter has travelled 4.5 years to reach us at this very instant…"

"This very moment the light is being reflected from this planet to the Cosmos. When do you think it will reach the Centauri?"

Nicholas did not think this was a difficult question and responded quickly:

"Since both are light beams and it arrives here in 4.5 years, then ours should reach there in 4.5 years from now."

The Old Man glanced with his warm fatherly smile at Nicholas:

"Correct. Fine… If we are seeing the light which left Centauri 4.5 years ago, what would an observer there looking at us today will see?"

"Light which had left us 4.5 years ago…"

"Yes. Correct logic. Laws of nature and laws of physics necessitate that…"

The Old Man was now firmly focused on Nicholas:

"In that case we would have seen through a powerful telescope the details of Centauri as it was 4.5 years ago. Is this not so?"

Nicholas, with a moment's hesitation, responded respectfully:

"Yes, Sir".

"If then the observer on Centauri was to look at this holy basilica, Hagia Sophia, with his powerful telescope, what would he see? You and me, or something else?"

Nicholas had to think on this one for a moment or two during which there was absolute silence covering the distant sounds of the city. He took his time, but he was careful not to make the Sage wait for a second more than necessary:

"Sir, the light reflecting from Hagia Sophia will reach there in 4.5 years, so the observer there will not see us at this very moment".

The Old Man appeared pleased with the progress Nicholas was making. He spoke with the gentle smile which always delighted and relaxed Nicholas.

"Good... carry on... what will he see this very moment?"

Nicholas careful not to faulter, pulled his concentration together, stopped a moment, and then he replied:

"I think he will see what was here 4.5 years ago. He would have seen Hagia Sophia as it was 4.5 years ago... perhaps the empty garden we are on now if there were no one here then..."

The Old Man was guiding him with questions toward a mystery as usual and helping him understand. They were moving together step by step... It was as if a father helping a son learn without any fears...

The Old Man leaned forward to the table again and said, "exactly". "In that case, if the observer on Centauri was to look at your sister's home in Jacksonville this very moment, would he have seen your 5 year old nephew?"

Nicholas was shocked to hear that the Sage knew about his nephew or the location of his sister's town. But he was in no position to question how he knew about it. He concentrated on the question posed to him.

"Sir, I think he will see the junior Cotrell as he was 5 or 6 months old..."

Nicholas was forced to answer thinking things through. He wasn't certain where this chat about the Cosmos was heading. He did not fall apart with an incorrect answer. He knew that this conversation was clearly leading to a climax of some type. The Sage still had his eyes firmly fixed on Nicholas. Still smiling on the opposite side of the table, he posed another question:

"You've mentioned your interest in documentaries. Tell me… Since each star is located at a different spot in the volume of Cosmos, are there not different stars whose lights reach us at longer and various periods?"

Without any delay, Nicholas said "Yes, Sir, there are…"

"Of course there are… millions of them although from here we can see only hundreds… Nicholas, do you know Hipparchus?"

This was a name Nicholas hadn't heard before. Nicholas had to admit his lack of knowledge:

"I'm sorry, Sir, but I don't know that name"

"Hipparchus, lived in Nicaea not too far from here just a little before Jesus' time… Nicaea is now called Iznik, a beautiful little town few hours from here on a lakeshore, where the famous Council was held to recompile different versions of the Bible together… In your concept of time, Hipparchus lived 400 years before that Council… It is also the town where one of the first big churches was erected after the Council was successfully concluded… Do you know, Nicholas? In that church there is a smiling depiction of our Lord Jesus… The only one in the world… Everywhere else he is depicted sad and sorrowful, but in Iznik he is smiling… A blessed smile… I learned how to smile from him in Jerusalem… The church was discovered by archeologists just before the time of Apollo Moon trip. When the depiction was first uncovered from behind a brick front closed compartment of the church wall, when that smile saw the day light for the first time over a millennium, it was as if the sign of wonderful things to follow... It was like a new hope followed shortly thereafter with the Moon landing of humanity... "

He stopped for a moment to catch his breath and perhaps thinking of an old friend:

"Well, back to Hipparchus... He lived prior to that church's construction and sadly never knew of Jesus. He used to stand on the outer defensive high walls of the town at late nights and observe the clear, fresh, pure night sky and chart the stars which we were able to see more distinctly than now. Mankind ruined so much... Even the stars are now locked behind a haze of air pollution... He was also one of our chosens... and charted trigonometrically and accurately over the many years 1500 main stars and constellations with his bare eyes. This is like a water droplet in an ocean. God's creation is beyond anyone's comprehension at the moment... We liked him... made him the first scientific astronomer of the western world... That is when humanity on this side of the world first started to conceptualize the Cosmos and began asking better informed questions. Naturally, finding some meaningful answers took more than a millennium in your time.... Secrets must be searched Nicholas... *Those who seek shall find* is the teaching of Jesus... And yet, so little is known by humanity... Isn't that so?"

Ensuring that Nicholas understood this minor diversion and without waiting Nicholas' answer he continued:

"Of course there are thousands and millions of stars and much more than anyone can see.... Hold your thumb up in the air against the sky, Nicholas..."

Nicholas was surprised at the command. He immediately did as he was told and held his hand up against the night sky as if giving an OK sign at a childhood baseball game... or as he used to salute his buddy Michael after a successful client meeting...

The Old Man added:

"You see the size of the night sky your thumb nail covers?"

"Yes, Sir."

"Well... hold your hand there steady... do not move.. In terms of the cosmic scales of God, the entire cosmos men is able to see and observe today with most advanced instruments, is just about as big as the space hidden behind your thumb nail... very small, very insignificant, is it not?"

Awed, Nicholas simply said "Yes..."

The Old Man continued:

"The light you see from each of the stars above has left their sources at different times. They all reach us at time periods expressed not only in human years, but in light years... Extremely long, incomprehensible lengths of time... Light is continous and it reaches us here... The source is always bright and shedding light nonstop. For example, the light of the northern polar star Polaris reaches us in 432 years.. It is 65 years for Aldebaran at the constellation Taurus. But light of Andromeda Galaxy, nearest to this solar system in what you call Milky Way, reaches here nearly in 3 million of your years. Well then... what about an observer at a location whose light reaches us in 90 or so years... What will he see? Suppose they are looking at the continent of Europe... What will they see?"

Nicholas thought a little to compute the year corresponding to about 90 years ago... He was good with numbers so he quickly replied:

"Sir, about 90 or so years ago, they would have seen the insane war in Europe... Yes... They would have seen the cruel delirium of humanity... The Big War in Europe, Sir, we call it the First

World War... millions upon millions died for no reason whatsoever... Sir.."

The Old Man approved, "Good" he said smiling, "...you are coming along very nicely", and continued:

"Alright, what would they see if they were observing us from a location whose lights reach us in about 75 years or so?"

Nicholas having figured it simply said, "The Second World War of 1940s, Sir."

The Old Man suddenly stood up with an agility one would not expect. He gestured at Nicholas to remain seated. Approached Nicholas, bent forward to his ear, and softly asked:

"Think well before you answer. What could those observers see? Can you tell me if those images will be still as in photographs or be something else?"

Nicholas wasn't expecting this one. It was much harder to put this question into a perspective. He recalled looking at Google Earth* at his office as he was planning his trips. He considered the Moon and Mars... Recalled his childhood experience at school with his science teacher who used to organize evening student trips for planetary observation with a large portable telescope. He recalled the chilly nights until they got a clear image of Jupiter's rings which appeared so small. He remembered his teacher telling him that the light from the Moon took 1 minute and 25 seconds to reach the Earth. This meant that he could observe astronaut movements made a minute and 25 seconds ago. He would observe all motion uninterrupted, but always after minute and twentyfive seconds later than the actual motions. So he took a chance and responded looking at the Old Man standing tall above him.

"Sir, I think they would have seen motion and movement. And they would have accepted the images as the movements and motions of the present time if they did not know the light travelling time as we do. They would have taken it as the reality of the moment..."

The Old Man simply responded saying, "Bravo... Exactly..." and walked back to his seat at the table. To make his point further, the wise man added:

"In that case, they could, for instance, conclude that the wars are going on and people warring are alive... and, yet we know that we lost those people... These people are dead in our time but still alive according to the observer unaware of *light years* at a different place in God's Cosmos..."

Nicholas froze for a moment.. He had never been told anything like this in his circles. Perhaps it was well known among those well versed on the subject. But not by the ordinary men on the street... The logic was obviously correct. Our world's *time* and the time of another place in the universe had different values of perception and imagery...

The Old Man was now waiting for Nicholas' response with his chin in his hand and with eyes fixed on his young friend's eyes. A few moments later, the sage voice was like the messenger of new secrets...

"If observers nearly 1985 or so years distant looked at Jerusalem, what would they have seen with their extremely powerful and sensitive telescopes?"

The answer was clear... Nicholas simply uttered softly:

"They would have seen Jesus..."

The Sage continued with great certainty:

"And in real... alive... in the flesh and bones... alive and preaching..."

Then he turned his gaze back to the night sky. Nicholas was now transported to a different dimension of perception... Preconceptions and assumptions in his mind were shaking from the roots. There was a silence until the Old Man began talking again.

"No... There is no such thing as fixed and constant time covering the entire universe.. It is all in the perception of an observer. In fact, in this cosmos, everyone is alive and well all at the same time. There is no past nor a future. Only the moment we perceive... Nicholas, I want you to know that humanity has made much progress toward discovering some secrets of God. For example, the recent concepts of *Quantum Physics* are a step forward. But, they are on the wrong path... They assume a *constancy of time* accross the universe. Of course there are multiple universes, many civilizations near and far... There is nothing in this obvious conclusion which should be surprising. Parallel universes, worm holes, black holes, big bang, etc. etc... It will take more time to sort these things out... Secrets are not to be had easily. They should be deserved... Why would God limit himself to a single universe? Is it not as simple as saying '...be', and there it is. Your science is still very much in its infancy... Scientists play with numbers and where they are unable to take it any further. They provide speculations and conjectures... The idea that one could be one thing in one universe and another at another universe... No... The reality is different... Each being is only in several universes of its own... None is allowed to be everywhere... There are millions of universes where we will never be... At this moment, in one universe Hitler is attacking France, in another your Founding Fathers are writing their declaration. Yet in another Genghis Khan is about to take China... In another, the faithful disciples of Jesus are seeking the Man Carrying Water Jug in Jerusalem to point the house of the last dinner. And this Old Man is now conveying special knowledge to a young chosen man in another universe…"

Garden conversation beside the mysterious Basilica under the starry dark night was continuing with mesmerizing concepts. Nicholas was absorbed in totally. He felt an incredible affinity and respect for the Sage who had taken him under his wings. He did feel chosen and special regardless of the stresses incurred by this Journey. He was pulled right back in to the moment's reality when the Old Man suddenly continued:

"Amazement and wonder of this creation is incomprehensible. The concept of God is not a straightforward and simple idea. God cannot be described as human-like creatures residing in the Mount Olympus. God is not one who sits above, observes us, interferes in nothing and simply waits to reward or punish us. It is not possible to assign a form or an attribute to God. God's being cannot be conceived with mind… and… the life God constituted for us is beyond magical… Life is strange… Fate is not a predictable system of laws and rules by which it is operated in God's domain… Not at all like what some scientists or men of cloth claim... Humanity has been misled much... One cannot simplify it to things like, your life would have been different 'if you had chosen another option', 'if you had not married her', 'if you had done this or that'… Unlike what your quantum physics researchers assume, there is no parallel universe just beside you that you can switch into with a simple choice or decision.... In this particular universe, at this very moment, all the past times are alive depending on where you look from. Let me give you another secret, Nicholas... In this cosmos what you call reality, the perceptions of reality depends on your physical coordinates in space. This also applies to your world here. At this very moment on this planet, every being's reality is different from the next even though a concentric scale rules perception from meta to macro, from macro to micro, to infinitesimal and beyond... From beyond to beyond as if opposing tips of an endless line... Think on this, Nicholas... There exists a mega-rule governing concentricity of reality... different *reality* as in spheres within spheres in every direction.. Reality is very different depending on which sphere you are in and at what coordinate you are located... At this moment you and I have a reality that may appear as a common reality to an observer whose reality is different, at this moment everyone is on a different line which everyone calls *time*... but *time* is not a reality... at this moment an observer at a very far coordinate in universe is observing the dinosaurs that once walked this earth.. *time* is irrelevant...what is crucial and essential is *timelessness* "

When the Old Man stopped for a moment to rest and perhaps recollect his thoughts, he seemed to be focused on a particular coordinate in the night sky above Istanbul... He seemed to be very much at peace.

The distant sounds of the city seemed to have livened a little. "Just like New York" thought Nicholas... "A metropolis has to begin its day early... Everyone's reality is different even though we are in one city... every cities' reality is different even though they are on the same continent... every continent, every planet, every solar sytem and every galaxy has its own concentric spheres of reality...from beyond to beyond..." were a quick review of what he just heard from the Old Man who seemed to show signs of a little exhaustion... "It must be so difficult for him" thought Nicholas... "He has to simplify everything to my level of comprehension... it must be so difficult for him... I wonder all the other things he is forced to leave out from this teaching... There must be so much more. There must be... Even if I've been chosen, will I ever learn an iota of that collection of secrets? Perhaps this old Sage only knows a portion... was Da Vinci given the same information? ...or was he tasked for other duties and servitude? Perhaps no one is given all the secrets... even the prophets... perhaps all the universes that exist or have existed are simply minute coordinates of God's own unchallenged spatial reality...." Nicholas was pleased with himself and was greatly comforted with the progress he had made in understanding the Old Man... The quick review in his mind appeared to make great sense. It seemed to have an elegant logic. Trying to avoid disturbing the Sage, seated in front of him, he hesitantly caught a glimpse of the wise Old Man. The gaze of his eyes seemed to have focused on that bright distant star and his wrinkled face seemed to firm up as he tried even harder to focus... As if he was seeing a reality of a different time on that star...

"Think of the nights, the dreams you had... People do not pay much attention to their dreams... For example, there are no shadows in dreams... it has sounds, colors, motion...but no smells... you can walk on water or fly in air... People do not pay attention to their dreams or to what is invisible...."

As the Old Man was speaking to Nicholas, who by now was feeling as if he was being purified of his misplaced preconceptions, while hearing the every spoken word more clearly, was able to correlate his personal experiences with the dreams he consistently had since childhood. "True" he thought, "none of my repeating dreams had any smells or shadows..."

He looked at the Old Man still focused on the same star. He wanted to hear more... Now Nicholas seemed to have developed an insatiable desire for more truths... Unlike his apprehensions and fears of the last few days and more, now he was far away from those disturbing questions and suspicions... He wondered if this was what the Old Man really meant when he spoke of the destruction of prejudices. He also felt that the Old Man was conducting this teaching in small portions as if to allow him to absorb the words spoken... He felt in the presence of a great teacher and was humbled again... Nicholas did feel that he was going through a very rapid self-transition from ignorance to wisdom... Felt more reassured with the wider and deeper comprehension and understanding he began to achieve... When he heard the Old Man's voice again, he knew instantly that the time to absorb what was said a few silent moments ago had come. He immediately concentrated fully on what was coming...

"At a certain moment during sleep, all universes converge and become unified... A single moment is experienced... At that moment all the past and future combine into one... become integrated... So at that moment all from past and present come together... There is no *time* at that moment. That is the moment called a *dream... dreaming...* Some remember their dreams very well and some do not for various reasons... But invariably everyone dreams... They may sense that they have experienced a dream but might not recall... Not like you... You always recalled your specially designated dream with all of its details... This was one of the criteria for choosing you... You did see me well... It was during that convergence you and I defied *time* and were united... and repeatedly... All creatures and creations of God dream at that moment of convergence. It is not necessarily a dream like a series of images or sounds... I do not know how, for example, trees or ants experience dream but I know they cannot remain outside of the *Convergence*. This is a convergence ordained by God..."

When the Old Man stood up quickly after his last words, it appeared that the conversation on *time, universes, reality, dreams* and *universal truths* was over... Nicholas, too, stood up immediately and followed him politely and respectfully. He now felt that finally they reached a true teacher and disciple relationship. He felt very secure and protected... a feeling which he did not have since childhood... They were now at the darkest moment of the night just before dawn. As they approached the front of Hagia Sophia, the Old Man's voice interrupted the silent walk through the night which seemed like an eternity devoid of time...

"Nicholas, research well and you will see that under normal circumstances all creatures die in their sleep... Some are very aware of the details of the dream's universe. They do take an astral journey... Some even spend extended times in those astral journeys. Some do establish kingdoms and domains in the astral cosmos..."

Upon ending his words the Man Carrying a Water Jug turned around and looked piercingly at Nicholas and held him by the shoulder with a gentle shake as if to bring Nicholas back into this reality he said, "think on these well... resolve the secrets of the astral world given to you..."

Then, he walked slowly taking support from the sidewall of the Basilica which also stood there as if it was impervious to the *passage of time...*

They stopped at the entrance section of Hagia Sophia. The Old Man looked up at the sky to the same spot... He looked like a statue when he was gazing at that star. He stayed motionless for an extended period. He was smiling affectionately at the star... as if in love...

"Nicholas, the light you see there is thought to be a star by everyone... even by the experts you have... It even has a popular name known by almost everyone... But let me tell you... That is neither a star nor a planet... that is a passage in space... it is light which pierces the space... an incredible beam from a wonderfully magnificent source... That is the location where it all started... That is where all will go when they depart this mega-reality which everyone calls the Planet Earth...."

Nicholas was looking in amusement at that brilliant star he had known since childhood. He was astonished by what he had heard. All seemed too unbelievable. He felt the spell of light piercing the night sky. At the entrance of Hagia Sophia, two silhouettes motionless, while looking at that bright spot thought to be a star, the Sage continued his hypnotizing explanation:

"People are unable to discern it from bright stars because it beams through the thick dark fabric like the others. Everything in the Cosmos, all galaxies, planets, our world, our sun, and all creatures of this Earth receive their life energy from that source which is assumed to be a star."

Nicholas came to himself with the Old Man's touch on his shoulder. He was absorbed in the bright spot and what he was hearing. The Sage headed to the basilica entrance as he said: "let's go in".

They entered in silence. The only sounds which can be heard were footsteps and the gentle swashing of water in the jug carried by the Old Man. As they walked through the gate opening to the main hall, the voice of the Sage began echoing:

"The constancy of the distance between the Sun and the planet Earth necessary for sustenance of life here, lack of sudden collision among the galaxies or planets are all due to the power of that darkness-puncturing bright spot assumed to be a star. Consider the fact that systems not sustained by an external force cannot remain stable for long and continue its presence for an extended period… No input, no output… Scientists of your day are claiming ideas which they are unable to comprehend themselves, things like, 'Big Bang created so much energy that the Cosmos is still expanding and the underlying forces are ensuring the motions of objects in space'. These are silly ideas when one considers the order in which Cosmos is arranged. Some of these scientists are far too vocal about what they claim to be a near-infinite big explosion. But, they are unable to explain the source of original power causing such an explosion and release of such energy. Only that it was a big explosion... Fine... in that case what was that which exploded? Where did all that immense energy come from?"

Hagia Sophia appeared more mysterious than ever with the minimal interior lighting. Nicholas felt as if the time had come to a full stop. He was listening to the Old Man in awe:

"In that case, I ask you... Why the corona of the Ssun is unbelievably hotter than its surface which is estimated to be around 6 thousand degrees? What is the reason? If the sun is generating heat within and discharging it outward, how could this be? Could it be that the corona is many thousands fold hotter because it receives power from a magnificent external source?"

Nicholas knew instinctively that these questions were not for him to answer right away. These were small pieces of information given to him for future consideration. This was the speech mannerism of the Sage. He kept following and listening silently as the Wise Man headed to the left section of the massive hall. They arrived at the left most main column known as the 'perspiring pillar'. The Old Man rested against it and said:

"Cosmos is so voluminous that numbers are insufficient to express its size. The distances among galaxies are stated in terms of light years. But this does not mean that universe is infinite in size or endless... Now pay attention... I will now give you knowledge which will change the World. Information which will change all technology and life on Earth..."

Nicholas was tensed up waiting to learn one of the most profound secrets of existence:

"Cosmos is not endless. On the contrary, it has boundaries and a certain geometry. Universe is in the form of a rectangular prism. But numbers do not suffice to express its size. Even terms like *trillion light years* fall very short of reality. However, it is not boundless or endless. That center of power which everyone thinks as a star pierces the universe at the exact center and passes through. This power is the beginning of everything and it provides the form and energy of universe. This force originates from a water source beyond the universe and radiates to entire cosmos…"

Nicholas immediately sensed that what was being said annulled and threw into thrash all that is known to be true about the universe. He did not know how to react other than with a perplexed look to the mischievous smile of the Sage...

When the Old Man said, "What are you thinking? Go ahead say something..." Nicholas stuttered... "I don't know what I could say, Sir. My mind is unable to grasp it all… Sir... this seems identical to the rejection of the belief which claimed that the world rested on the horns or in a tray on the back of an ox... It is tantamount to the idea that the world is a globe floating in space." The Old Man was pacing extremely slowly around the pillar caressing it with his hand as he spoke:

"I understand… This was never said before… The World evolved technologically in the last century. This was in part due to discovery of facts not previously known about the Cosmos. How did this happen? Is this not interesting?"

While saying these, the Sage once again wore his mischievous but affectionate smile. Nicholas carefully continued to listen, standing a few small steps away from the Perspiring Pillar. The Old Man stopped suddenly. He removed the cup lid off the jug and began pouring water from the famous column hole down the pillar surface. Not too long ago Nicholas had stopped here during a day visit and had stood in line with tourists anxious to see this pillar cavity which served as a wishing well. It is believed that a full counter clockwise rotation of the hand with thumb in the cavity actualized any wish one might have. Nicholas also had tried it. But now the Old Man was carrying out another ritual. He turned a full circle around the column while pouring water and quickly turned to Nicholas:

"You will be given a book downstairs. That book reveals all the information necessary to prove what I've told you so far about the bright spot in the night sky and the geometry of the universe. Make sure that you forward these methods to the appropriate people... It is now time for new discoveries... A new era must begin... It is necessary to alter the direction in which humanity is going... New instruments are needed. Like one of our chosen ones, Tesla had understood well that the universe had boundaries. But his life was cut short..."

The Old Man put his right hand thumb in the pillar cavity and uttered in a low voice several incomprehensible sentences. The Old Man's body was tense against the column and appeared as if pushing the pillar. While Nicholas was trying to grasp what was happening, the small gentle lights of Hagia Sophia interior blinked several times. As Nicholas tried to see in shock what was happening around him, he caught a glimpse of the Old Man taking two forceful steps slowly revolving the pillar. Nicholas was amazed. The thumb of the Old Man was still in the column cavity as he stepped forward in difficulty. As he revolved, the famous Perspiring Pillar which appeared to be a supporting pillar of the Basilica rotated with the Old Man generating a loud noise which violently echoed in the hall. Just as the pillar neared its full turn, a very loud terrifying metallic chain noise from somewhere up above and the noises of stone frictions echoed ferociously. Just as Nicholas turned suddenly to see what was happening, all the lights in the entire hall went off. With blinding darkness set, all the noises also diminished and disappeared. Before he could even adjust his vision to the pitch black, he heard the Old Man say:

"Stay calm, do not fear… Hold my hand. Never let it go…"

Nicholas felt the soft and warm reassuring hand of the Sage. It was as if the hand of a loving father. That's exactly how Nicholas felt in the scary circumstances. He also sensed that they were stepping forward diagonally. He was still unable to see in darkness, but inherently trusted the Sage and held his hand firmly. After a short walk in silent darkness, the Jug Carrier started to talk about new mysteries as if wanting to calm Nicholas down:

"Nicholas… Do you realize that fate works in secretive ways? If you concentrate on worthwhile and useful, helpful beneficial things and sincerely hope for such, God will create chances for you in ways unimaginable. It will eventually come your way so long as you are prepared in advance.

The order of events is preordained but it is not known to us who will be tasked with it. For example, discovery of a technology which will recover from space the voices of those who are long deceased is preordained but we do not know who will be honored with this discovery. The World's fate dictates and requires such advancement. But no one knows who the inventor will be… Someone who devoted himself to such a subject for years will be given the task and the honor. Others will simply say 'he just made a discovery and became wealthy and famous'… But the secret is preparedness, devotion and healthy thought dedicated to the betterment of the planet and its residents… Devotion and contribution with sincerity without material expectations or fame is the key… Humble and genuine respect for the God-given intellect, modesty and hard work… Seek and you shall find…

For example a new form of intercontinental transportation technology which will reduce the travel time between your country and Istanbul to less than 30 minutes... For this to happen space must be better understood and its finite nature must be realized... This will eventually happen. But it is not yet known who will see this light first. We do not yet know the name of that person... One must be ready and prepared to assume the role God will assign... Without a healthy and sound mind, it is impossible to reach any significant and meaningful, long lasting objective. And without honest prayers and noble wishes which deserve honor, no desire will ever materialize…"

The wise voice of the Sage, what he was hearing and the steps taken in pitch darkness made Nicholas feel like he was flowing in some strange world and time. A mixture of curiosity and trepidation had enveloped him. A tall and robust looking column in the temple hall rotated with a great noise and the whole place was submerged into darkness. They were walking in a temple much older than a thousand years. Erected in the early days of Christianity… It seemed as if they were at some unfamiliar coordinate of the Cosmos… Completely detached from realities... The Old Man had mentioned the book to be given below the temple... Did he mean the large water pond with those Egyptian hieroglyphics? Who would be giving the book? While Nicholas was walking with these questions on his mind, he heard the startling command "Stop". He stopped dead on his track.

The Old Man instructed him by saying, "Lower your head. We will pass through a small gate. Don't hit your head." Nicholas bent quite low and took a step. As his arm swiped the stone sidewall, he sensed that he passed through something.

After entry, he was finally able to vaguely see the stairs heading down. The spiral stairs were taking them down with the Jug Carrier leading the way.

The voice of the man was reheard:

"Nicholas... I told you about the star... the centre of the universe... Do not forget... It originates and passes through water beyond the universe. Remember three quarters of this planet is water... in its many forms water surrounds us even as vapor in the atmosphere... Our bodies are composed mostly of water... We live in a very watery, water dominated life... Think about this... and think well..."

After many minutes Nicholas felt that the stairs just did not end. It was clear that they were far below the upper main hall. He estimated that they must have walked down about 200 steps. The Old Man's voice was very sharp in the corridor of the stairway.

"Living beings cannot sustain thirst for long. All living creatures require water. Some a little sooner, some a little later.. But eventually thirst must end either by water or death... With the exception of dry bones, everything contains some amount of water... Why doesn't dry bone contain water? This is another secret... There is incredible force and mystery in this..."

Finally the long climb down the spiral stairs ended. They reached a wide and flat landing. The place was cavernous. Ahead, there were two large alcoves which stood like medieval castle gates.. But neither alcove appeared to have much depth. It appeared like they had reached the end of the road. It did not seem there existed any other place they could go. Nicholas wondered if this was the place where he would be given the book. He looked questioningly at the Jug Carrier. At that moment the previous ritual of sprinkling water to the sidewall to their right was repeated with water from the jug. Then the Old Man inserted his finger to what appeared to be a cavity. The wall of the cavern slid open sideways with loud noise. This did not surprise Nicholas. They entered from the opening at the sidewall. An inclined corridor pathway was barely visible. The Sage led the way with Nicholas in tow. He was hearing the echoes of the touching voice of the Sage who sounded very tired:

"Life exists with water… On this planet nothing can remain alive indefinitely without water… Because God has bestowed powers on water."

The Old Man suddenly stopped and turned to Nicholas:

"Do you know that human thrown into water does not sink? But when you add the suspicion and fear of sinking to the body, it becomes heavier than water and sinks… I wonder if you ever realized that learning swimming is only a momentary trust in water without any hesitations. All is created from water… Water does not allow sinking of what has been created from it… and holds it at surface… "

Then the Sage slowly bent down and put the water jug on the floor. He sat on the floor. Gestured at Nicholas to sit down. There was a sharp smell of seaweed and a weak humming noise in the background. They were taking a well-deserved short break. He took the cup off the water jug and added some water into it. He drank it slowly in small sips with eyes closed and took a breath after each sip. After finishing his water, he said nothing nor did he offer any to Nicholas. He placed the cup on the jug and slowly stood up. Then he said:

"Do not be offended. I hope you are not very thirsty. At the moment I shan't be offering you any water."

"Thank you Sir. I am not thirsty at the moment."

He was actually quite thirsty. But they continued down the inclined pathway. At the end of it, they stepped down the four short stairs. It was still pitch dark everywhere, but there was a weak light. But the Jug Carrier lit a match and a small torch on the sidewall came aflame. The torches located a little further were also lit. Then came the light. Nicholas was near frozen stiff. This was a very large spatial place. The walls were carved to shelves. Thousands of books were on the shelves. The main hall opened to smaller caverns and they, too, were filled with books on the shelves. While admiring this huge library carved off from rock under the basilica, the Old Man Carrying a Water Jug spoke as he too was viewing the book piles on the shelves:

"Do you know Nicholas, once a great physicist screamed at a symposium saying that 'only 30 books survived Andalusia… and so we split the atom… If half of the million books destroyed there had survived, we could have been travelling amidst galaxies now'. He was screaming a just truth to the whole world."

As he was speaking, he was also lovingly caressing the books nearest to him. The sadness in his eyes were reflected in his voice.

"If Baghdad, Alexandria and Cordoba was spared destruction or if the libraries were not destroyed after conquest... if these libraries were inherited by humanity… the travel to Mars would have been a common thing today... The loss of those libraries is one of the greatest tragedies of humanity throughout its known history... Humanity was set back thousands of years with the loss of that knowledge accumulated over many millennia…"

The Jug Carrier stood saddened beside the ancient books. He caressed each one he could reach as if caressing a tender rose. Nicholas followed slowly with momentary stops at every few steps to permit the Old Man affectionately touch the books. Finally, they arrived at an entrance of another spiral stairway heading down. Within a short time, they were confronted with a large hall about the size of the upper one. The walls were covered with ancient Egyptian hieroglyphics. Among the figures he noticed the prominence of a painting depicting the combat of Cyclops and a man. Walls also contained two cat sphinxes which appeared to be supporting the cavernous ceiling. The Old Man and Nicholas walked futher down the hall. Upon reaching another entrance, the Old Man cautioned him pointing at the stairway: "Be careful… Very slippery… Hold on to me. It is going to be a long way down…"

Nicholas' first step slid. He avoided falling by leaning against the wall. The stairway was very unusual. It was actually inclined flooring with a step carved in stone every two or three steps. A narrow, seaweed smelling humid corridor of hazards… Nicholas wondered how deep beneath the basilica they were and why this corridor did not have a more proper stairway. At least like the ones they've just been through…Walking on it was very dangerous. It appeared like an intentional design… Nicholas remembered reading in a history book about a castle built by the Knights of Malta during the European Crusades of the 11th and 12th Centuries. The book had explained the strange arrangement of walls and flooring in the corridors of defensive walls. These floorings were inclined in such a way to instantly disorient anyone who was unfamiliar with the corridors and lacked practice. He also recalled how The Knights of Malta eventually became a very secretive and influential organization affecting the affairs of Europe in the Middle Ages. While Nicholas was following the old Sage, his mind was running wild, triggered with the mystery of his circumstances, he heard the unexpected warning: "Nicholas… This walk is going to take time. Do not occupy your mind with questions and what you see… Listen carefully to what I am about to say…"

Nicholas responded immediately: "Of course, Sir"... The strange humming he had heard in the background on the previous floor became increasingly more noticeable. He listened to the echoing voice of the Sage:

"Your biophysicists are investigating the life force in living beings. They are interested in the pure energy and not so much the material organics. This is correct and justified. What they have seen is that water and salt are the basis of the source of all thought processes. Your neuroscientists have clearly identified and demonstrated that your brain neurons operate with very low electricity. Without water as well as several other essential minerals, there can be no sound thought process. Your physicians finally understood the importance of water and trace minerals... Now they strongly advise generous water intake daily and affirm the importance of various salts in brain and body functions. Nicholas... Do you know? This country has the richest naturally occurring mineral hot water springs in the world. A large variety of them which help heal many different ailments. Nicholas... You should consider worldwide advertisement of this fact... It will be a good deed done by you for the entire humanity..."

Nicholas was astonished and pleased when the Old Man brought miracles of water together in one breath with the most incredible idea of worldwide advertising. He was amazed beyond description by the knowledge and fluidity of his Sage's mind. How he connected one thing to another like a fine needle work of an expert grandmother... Not choosing to respond to any of the questions seemingly requiring an answer, he continued to listen silently:

"Nicholas... One must drink variety of waters not simply to become physically healthy but rather for health of mind and for extended consciousness... Don't ever forget these words... Our bodies do not store water in a special organ designed for that purpose alone. Water must at all times be provided externally. But too much of it may not be helpful... Everything in moderation without any excess, Nicholas... Moderation is an important quality which brings you closer to God. Water is a natural therapy. One must always have some available... One must drink a reasonable amount every day."

Nicholas noticed that there seemed to be a regular sequence of stair steps followed by a gently inclined flat surface landing... He thought it might be a sequence of every dozen or so steps and a landing which after a short walk led to another set of steps... There seemed to be a rhythm, but Nicholas also felt uneasy about the details with which he was intermittently occupying his mind contrary to the earlier cautionary instructions given to him. He was laso delighted with the Old Man's light hearted muse referring to advertisement. Nicholas knew that the Man Carrying a Water Jug clearly saw through his soul, but never indicated any such powers. Perhaps not to scare him. Meanwhile the Old Man had confidently increased his pace down the corridor as if to encourage Nicholas to do the same and continued to speak:

"Each water molecule is different. Each molecule is nothing but a perfect structure with 104.7 degrees. Don't ever forget this. That beam of light, that majestic power passes through water and spreads to the Cosmos. Universe is prismatic. Water too has a similar structure. Grasp this concept well... This geometry present in the molecule bestows on water a very specific frequency characteristic. A water molecule has dual polarity. Just like this planet... North and south poles... Each water molecule has a magnetic field with negative and positive polarity.

Since water has polarities, it is subject to certain gravitational and lift forces. Water has a gravitational force. Water flows downward. As a substance with chemical and physical properties, while water flows downward, it also flows upward as pure energy of light. All forms of matter are nothing but frozen and slowed down versions of energy. Energy is the substance of matter..."

The Sage stopped at the same time with his last word. Turned to Nicholas and cautioned: "Think well on these words... I am revealing the secrets of water to you... Listen very well... See the mighty power of water. Grasp fully what it can do and use it."

Nicholas nodded firmly and quickly to indicate his full acceptance of the warning just given. The nodding of his head so voluntarily and convincingly must have been sufficient for the Old Man who had kept his piercing eyes on Nicholas. Turned back and stepped forward into the darkish stairs with Nicholas right behind him. Nicholas kept silent as he followed attentively. The humid and narrow passage allowed them through in the midst of increasing humming like a distant roar beyond the walls. The silence of the journey with careful steps taken downward continued until the Old Man decided to end it abruptly while gently buffing his hand on the surface of the humid wall:

"There is not a single ailment without a cure... In principle, all problems, whatever they may be, have treatments hidden among the secrets of the Universe... The fundamental question is whether we have sufficient knowledge and understanding or not... A physician may say he is helpless in providing a successful treatment. What he is admitting is that he doesn't have the knowledge... When an ailment surface in an organ, if we can return it to its original harmonious energy, then the organ will adapt naturally... It will return to its natural state... This would happen very simply. With water and various mineral salts... Remember we are all derived from water... Water is perfect... It absorbs almost anything when given time... Provided there is sufficient time... and patience combined with good will... sincerity... Everyone must drink water in the manner I showed you... Each droplet... each sip must be appreciated as a gift of God... Human body, like the bodies of all other living beings has immense capacity for self-healing... Water has a purifying effect. It is the primary influent on the bodies of all living beings. Water has a simple but superior form endowed by God with special powers... It must be respected, preserved and used in appreciation of its divine nature. It is a magnificent gift from Heavens beyond this universe. These powers must be discovered and utilized."

Nicholas was listening with great care and in the meantime watched his steps to prevent a foolish fall on the wet stone flooring... The Old Man stopped once again... This was not surprising. They were afoot for a long time in environments which Nicholas perceived as being somewhat stressful. The Old Man carefully placed his jug on the floor and sat beside it with his back leaning against the corridor stone wall. Nicholas was not late in joining him but this time he was simply kneeling in anticipation that the Sage may quickly rise again. It seemed easier just to kneel next to the Old Man. There was between them a warm relationship now... and Nicholas did not feel, nor did the Old Man indicated any sign of disrespect... Just as Nicholas leaned his back to the humid sidewall and settled in comfortably, still ready to give a hand to the Old Man should he decide to stand... Nicholas wanted to hold his hand like a loving son and assist him to stand easily... The Sage appeared relaxed as he began talking:

"Water dissolves in it all evil and goodness... Water prefers goodness and suppresses evil... it blesses... This is the real reason why babies should be baptized with water... Not because they are the product of a sinful process like some mistakenly think or they are blemished at birth. They should be baptized with pure water because they are the gift of God filled with goodness. Because water contains the goodness of God... This is why even adults were baptized with water by our brother John The Baptist... He understood the God-given power of water. This is why our Jewish brothers also value water. This is why our Muslim brothers ensure compliance to *abdhest* (ritual ablution) with clean water prior to each daily prayer... Did you not see the ablution fountains in mosque gardens today, Nicholas? I like how our Muslim brothers do it... I do the same... I enjoy the ritual of refreshing my soul just like devout Muslims do in ablution. Slowly absorbing the power of water... in sequence... with a momentary interval between every move of the ritual... just like sipping water followed with a breath in between... Enjoying and appreciating every drop of the water in humility... The feeling of cleanliness and coolness of chilly water I enjoy. Its wet feeling and softness... its sounds as it pours out of the fountain... When with water, Nicholas... I feel closest to God... I am always reminded of God's unyielding and infinite powers. This is one of the reasons why I always carry water with me...Water cleanses and purifies. It sheds the toxins out of one's body and soul."

The Sage's incredible ability to put everything so easily into perspective transported Nicholas from one spiritual orbit to another effortlessly. These wonderful pieces of knowledge being given beneath a historical temple in a not so bright corridor extending from a cavernous repository of ancient books was beyond all possible imagination of a mortal...

As the Old Man made an effort to rise, Nicholas was quick to hold his hand and assist him... His alertness was welcomed by the Sage who rewarded him with a loving glance of appreciation. Nicholas felt very comforted and warm. He was very happy.... a feeling which he did not experience before. He felt he reached at that moment a very special standing in the eyes of the Man Carrying a Water Jug. They began walking down the path which echoed again.

"Nicholas... Human body contains in every direction fluid channels totaling ninety thousand kilometers carrying each day water-based liquids like the precious blood... Everyone knows that water easily curves on itself, often creates spirals and deep whirling... Just like what your scientists call the DNA... Interesting, huh?"

Nicholas suddenly caught the glimpse of water droplets seeping intermittently downward on the stone wall. He began to understand more fully that next to the destruction of prejudices at the rear garden of Hagia Sophia above, he had completed now another stage of mental purification several floors beneath the basilica at a humid dark corridor with water humming at the background louder than ever... sounded the humming of universe... wondered if the source of water beyond the Cosmos might have a similar steady happy song which accompanied God-endowed powers of goodness... Like the secrets of DNA which in itself is a product of water and proteins organized in a mysterious way... He understood now that water permeated everything... It was everywhere...

The Old Man's voice was occasionally enriched with his deep breath. In fact it was getting quite difficult to breathe comfortably where they were. Now the seaweed like aroma was more evident in the air. Nicholas thought that water was essential... just like air...

Breathing had become difficult where they were. The Man Carrying a Water Jug continued to speak with deep breath intervals as he stepped down the stairs:

"In reality, our respiration includes breathing water vapor in the air. We have been created from water and while not aware of it, we live in water. Snowflakes which are solid forms of water have been photographed by an electron microscope. Examine those pictures. They are perfect small hexagons. It is interesting that no two flakes are identical. For crystallization, more than one billion biophotons operate in each water molecule and these self-organize continuously. This causes each water molecule to be different from one another and have a unique identity."

The narrow and humid place made it difficult for the Old Man to breathe. Nicholas also felt the same way. When they stopped for a momentary rest, the Old Man was leaning on the wet wall with his hand trying to catch his breath. He looked at Nicholas as he spoke:

"Water, like the air, is the most fundamental need of an individual. Lack of water causes severe health problems. One of the main reasons for headache is dehydration. 90% of brain consists of water. For this reason the first signs of dehydration surfaces in brain functions. Most of the time headaches can be cured only by drinking water without the use of any medication.

As we get old our veins and brain synaptic connections are calcified. Dysmnesia occurs due to failure in bridging the synapses. Eventually Alzheimer's claws takes hold. The main issue here is dissolving the calcification. For this, one needs life, knowledge, structure and geometry of water. Only then you can break the molecule formations. To avoid Alzheimer's you must drink at least 2 liters of water each day in the manner I have instructed you. If you are suffering from Alzheimer's, then everyday you must drink constituted life water with proper geometry that is structured for this purpose."

After completing his words, the Sage waited for a brief period of silence. Nicholas was trying not only to grasp what was just told, but resolve the whole picture. He enjoyed learning such secrets. But what was the purpose of all this? Why were these being told to him? He felt crazed when he failed to find logical responses to the questions churning in his mind. While Nicholas was struggling with these thoughts, the Jug Carrier ended his brief rest and headed downward. After a few steps down the stairs, his mysterious voice echoed in the corridor.

"Nicholas... There are segmented diagnostic and organometric instruments. These can make measurements at the energetic level. These devices can prove that some diseases can be eliminated only by water.

Biophysicists know that human body can self-heal. Each organ has a different vibration characteristic because of the various combinations of elements. Vibration is almost the main law of Quantum Physics. You should try learning Quantum Physics. You should at least follow the developments. If you could peek into everything around you with an incredibly powerful electron microscope, you would see that all are constituted by energy resembling vibrating strings. In fact all that exists is a distinct energy. And... all energies are interrelated. What we call a material, a substance which can be handled is nothing more than energy in a state of inertia. Quantum physics saw this reality, and so the future will be very different. Your structural formation is nothing but vibrating strings of energy and each has a unique vibrational power.

For example, natural state vibration of a lung is about 40 Hertz. If you consume excessive alcohol or smoke your lung's vibration frequency may rise as high as 58 Hertz. When this happens, the material structure of the organ might be altered. This means deformation of the organ. This may not manifest itself all at once but will in time emerge as an ailment. Let us first remember that the level of energy changes. If one can readjust the energy vibration to its original natural state, then the cure and regaining health is possible.

When a patient with brain tumor is given water containing the vibrational frequencies missing in the body, you will see a very different picture. Within only 19 minutes the damaged places, epiphysial, hypophysis and central nervous system exhibit changes. But, having lived wrong all your lives, do not for a moment think that by drinking the miracle water which I shall reveal will cure in an instant. The patient will slowly return to the original state, but because the body has been so accustomed to the ailment condition, it will take more than several hours. What you must conclude from this information is the availability of miraculous energy in water which reconstitutes the missing and causes rejuvenation. If you could provide 2 liters of miracle water daily to a patient, then during an extended period the diseased bodily structures will regain health."

When the wise words ended, there was a silence in the narrow passage heading down. Nicholas was stuck on the words '*the miracle water which I shall reveal*' thinking "of course, I knew there was a mystery... Da Vinci's book contained the script WATER on each page... No wonder the Old Man's name is not mentioned... Even the Bible refers to him as the Man Carrying a Water Jug... There must be something called miraculous water." In awe, Nicholas' excitement had peaked.

The relatively weak background roaring noise heard all along the corridor heading downward was now immense. The Sage added:

"Do not panic, Nicholas... what you are hearing is the bottom current of the Bosphorus. We are now beneath the sea channel".

This was unbelievable and terrifying. Nicholas was shocked in surprise and for the first time during their walk in the narrow stone humid passage he broke his silence and voiced his emotions by responding, "...we are beneath the sea which I had walked along today? .. Incredible! Fantastic!" Nicholas' voice contained all elements of a true and sincere awe. The roar was now even stronger. The Old Man stopped suddenly and leaned against the stone wall with his hand. "This is the sound of the Bosphorus... This is the voice of the secret hidden by the Bosphorus..." Then he began stepping down again while continuing to speak.

"In the Bosphorus above, the sea flows visibly from north to south. The reason for this is the elevation of the Black Sea, water level of which is higher than that of the Marmara Sea. But what eyes cannot see is that there is another current at the level where we are now which runs in the opposite direction from south to north toward the Black Sea. This is called the Bosphorus bottom current and it transports water hundreds of times larger than that of Niagara Falls with incredible force. This deafening roar you hear is the sound of the bottom current."

As he finished his words, they were on dry ground landing at the bottom of the stone wet stairs which took a long time to travel. The Sage walked fast as if he had to reach a destination. Nicholas followed him with his awe and fear intact. The stone passage suddenly became curved. The zigzagging pathway ended at a very bright room. Nicholas froze where he was. He looked around him in this bright and pleasant place. The light flowed in from the outside through the room windows. Light at the bottom of the sea...

This place looked like an area one might see in an amazing palace. There were very tall rectangular windows both on the right and left. Nicholas was amazed at the scenery seen from the windows. Outside was the sight of a magnificent city under water... It was such a beautiful sight that he hadn't noticed the ornamented gate ahead of him. There was a large human figure clearly the result of great mastery and workmanship. Nicholas recognized the figure's face at once. The face was that of the male depicted in the mosaic rendition of Da Vinci's woman now displayed at the Zeugma Museum. This mosaic was the inspiration for the Mona Lisa painting. Nicholas had seen this male figure face in the mosaic composition and thought "it might be Zeus". Later Nicholas had understood from Da Vinci's 'Book of Secrets' that this male depiction was of King Solomon. The embossed depiction on the incredible gate ahead of him was identical to what he had seen in that museum. King Solomon...

Nicholas was amazed and did not know what to say as he perused in awe his surroundings. It was the first time throughout the night where he felt no need to hear what the old Sage might say next. The carved scripts on the gate were magnificent specimens of the art of writing. Although he could not read what was written, he was absorbed in the beauty of letters. As he was focusing on the writings, he heard the mystical voice again. The Old Man was reading the script to Nicholas:

"Enter and fear thine justice not sought..."

The Jug Carrier smiled and pushed open the big door, saying "follow me". As Nicholas stepped in, he was shocked to see what he saw. An incredible structure ornamented with hundreds of pillars, with a geometrically dancing ceiling and beautiful arch decorations. The columns appeared to have a specific aesthetic and philosophical statement beyond their technical characteristics. It was as if those who ornamented the pillar heads in Hagia Sophia above had seen this place. This palace-like spatial place was reminiscent of an oasis in the desert and palm trees spreading along the oasis. The folded arches extending to both sides of a pillar looked identical to the branches and leaves of a palm tree. This was a majestic structure where culture, civilization, aesthetics, beliefs and philosophy were united... Arches of red and white stones... Workmanship of the thin golden motifs on the ceiling above were beyond perfection. The hall was fairly spacious. Rectangular large windows surrounded the place. Words could now have done justice in expressing the beauty of the city scenery outside. As Nicholas was looking in amazement and perplexed to the submerged city from one of the large windows, the Sage standing in the middle of the hall spoke:

"Welcome to Alinapolis ..."

Nicholas had a million questions to ask. After seeing this sight, he had no strength to conform to the prohibition imposed on him. But this Journey had become a very sweet, amazing pleasure. He did not want to deprive himself of any forthcoming knowledge by violating the ban on questions. While he was forced to wait for the Sage to say a few words, Nicholas kept murmuring to himself:

"Alinapolis... Incredible... Outstanding..."

The Old Man hearing this murmur came beside Nicholas and spoke as he also gazed at the submerged city.

"You are now at the hall of the famed Princess Alina Palace. Above us is the bottom current of the Bosphorus, above it is the sea and at the very top is a palace on the horn-like protruding land known as Sarayburnu (Seraglio Point) for many centuries. At one time they were an Empire of Water which reigned for 700 years and led the civilization. But inevitably they disappeared... The legendary continent lost and now discussed by everyone... the lost civilization... Atlantis..."

Nicholas looked at the Sage in total amazement when he heard the name 'Atlantis'. Was this the city of Atlantis, the civilization about which many books had been written? He had difficulty in comprehending the whole scene. It was unbelievable...

The Jug Carrier slowly and gently continued as he, too, was looking at the city with deep and thoughtful but vacuous gaze:

"This is Alinapolis... The capital of the lost continent Atlantis... The place referred to as Atlantis, the giant territory of Macedonia, began from here and included the mysteries of Zeugma and boundaries stretched to the Egypt of antiquity. What submerged into the water was not the continent of Atlantis. What got submerged to the bottom of the sea was Alinapolis, the brain and soul of Atlantis..."

Nicholas was bewitched and mesmerized with the sight of numerous palace-like magnificent structures standing submerged ahead of him. He was speaking to himself in a whisper, "Anyone would be breathless with the sight of this beauty... what a wondrous city..." Yes, this was absolutely true. Regardless of who or what they were, everyone would have been struck with this magical and mysterious beauty. It seemed Atlantisians preferred the best and the most glorious. It seemed that when they reached the peak of their civilizations, they did not hesitate to erect a legendary and a famed opulent palace... Nicholas couldn't help but think in any other way as he viewed the beauty of the palace in which he stood. Words did not suffice to express its beauty and uniqueness. No doubt this palace must have been the only reason why they called the horn like protruding small peninsula above the *Sarayburnu* for many centuries, the *Palacehorn or Seraglio Point as commonly known*, at the shoreline above.

The Sage looked at Nicholas and spoke thoughtfully:

"This is the gift of a most passionate love ever felt for a woman. This is the gift of King Solomon to his love Alina. Not only this palace, but all that you are able to see was built only for Alina, his love. He explained Water to all those whom he ruled. He showed

Water's power. He taught them how to yield that power. In this way an incredible empire, a civilization using unheard technologies emerged. The Empire of Water... The Mu.... In your words, the Atlantis..."

Nicholas paced slowly and silently forward toward the adjacent windows as if desiring to see from different angles the immense city submerged... As he peeked from the window on his right, he noticed the lights coming from strange structures which barely resembled the Egyptian pyramids... Yes... They were all under water, and, in so far as what he understood, this was the bottom of the Bosphorus. How was it possible that such depth would be lit so bright at night? What was the source of this light? How was the light spreading from these walls formed? How could there be light at the bottom of the sea? Should it not have been pitch darkness? These questions got the best of him and not being able to raise a question was absolute pain.

The Old Man smiled affectionately, but mischievously as if he had been reading Nicholas' mind:

"I know... You are pondering on the brightness here.... This light is the secret of Alinapolis. This is a secret given to them by Solomon. This is the most important secret which distinguishes their civilization. The system which lit their houses. Solomon taught them how to build using a special mixture of water, salt and soil. These structures stored the sun light and continuously released light. For this reason, there never was a time of darkness in Alinapolis. Every corner of Alinapolis was lit bright with the stored photonic energy. When a continental geophysical tragedy occurred and the waters of the elevated Black Sea surged on Alinapolis, the earth carried by the sudden flood formed a layer over the city... This was a ceiling of very thick clay quick mud over Alinapolis. Then... very strangely... the bottom current started flowing in the opposite direction from south to the northern

Black Sea. Eventually, the surface of the clay mud swamp hardened and formed the base of the Bosphorus. About a century later, another current formed from the Black Sea to the south. Then both currents in opposite directions continued ever since. The light you see now is formed by a whirling flow which enters from the mouth of a cavernous opening at the bottom of Bosphorus and which carries light absorbed by the crystalline walls you see over there... The walls built by the secret system revealed by King Solomon still brighten the city..."

The Sage seemed at ease as he gazed the city with his hands in the broadcloth attire. Then he turned suddenly to Nicholas, "Soon you, too, will discover this technology. There is intense research. There is a little way to go. They discovered that when the bubbles in water exploded with sound waves, they release light...But it is not understood yet... These walls absorb the light and release it..."

Nicholas did not understand how this could simply be explained by any form of light. The walls were crystalline. The light was absorbed by the crystals and later released in darkness. This was so amazing... People were able to light their environment thousands of years ago. Just like daylight...

As he continued to enjoy the miraculous city scenery standing in front of him, he caught a glimpse of the Sage depart and head toward the palm-like arches in the rear. He immediately moved and followed him with a great curiosity. The Old Man was walking toward a beautifully ornamented and decorated large table with something in his hand. Nicholas followed him wondering what it might be.

The Man Carrying a Water Jug sat silently at a chair near the table and and he was busy with the object in his hand. When Nicholas caught up with him, he saw that the object was something like an old radio. As if he had read Nicholas' mind, without raising his head the Old Man said, "this is not a radio... This is an invention which will sell like crazy around the world".

Nicholas looked in amazement. As the dial on it was turned, the amber light on its screen turned either green or red and weak squeaky sounds were heard from its speaker. Then all of a sudden when human voices, bird sounds and a vague music was heard, he shut off the strange device. Smiling, he raised his head and looked at Nicholas and said: "this is an invention which will enable hearing the voices who have passed away... I think of it as an invention which will allow hearing the voices of people living in the parallel universe... at the moment gigantic technology companies are spending millions to invent this, but they do not know where the voices are... When they learn that the universe is prismatic and understand that they must use water, then they will succeed..."

Nicholas, fairly surprised, found this statement a bit exaggerated, but he instantly recalled his childhood memory in which he took an imaginary phone everywhere in Jacksonville pretending to talk to his parents. Later the hand held tiny phones had become a reality. Why not this one? Nicholas kept looking at the device with a great curiosity.

The Sage turned on the device saying, "the voices you will hear in a moment are from the streets of ancient Alinopolis". As he increased the sound volume of the device, Nicholas felt as if he was traversing the time tunnel.

A composition of instrumental music filled the beautiful palace hall. He couldn't understand the human speeches heard. It seemed like a mixture of male and female voices in a busy market place. The sound of water pouring continuously, bird sounds and occasional cat meows in between... Sounds from thousands of years ago... fabulous... beyond wonders...

Nicholas was absorbed in the sweet sound of water and the harmony of peaceful music. He felt odd feelings... Alinapolis, the land of water... This glorious palace looking at the submerged city... Princess Alina's Palace... It was like a observation vista. The city was visible in most part... Nicholas seemed travelling back in time at a mystical lost city. While listening to the echoes emerging from the ages past, he began walking slowly to the left of the lengthy hall. He touched the columns which were once also caressed by King Solomon. The feeling shivered his body in chill. He had touched one by one to seventy pillars and reached the far left end window of the hall. What could be seen little ahead from the window was a big structure exhibiting the finest art workmanship. This was probably the entrance to the city. The large statutes of lions lined both sides of the road leading to the entrance. They stood as if they might come alive at any moment. There were two delicately ornamented giant pillars standing on two bulls. The pillars were connected overhead with a horizontal column with very beautiful scripts. And above all was a massive eagle with wings spread. As Nicholas paid attention to the writings, he sensed that the sounds from the device were coming closer. He turned back and saw the Sage coming toward him. When he reached near, Nicholas he began reading the script on the gate...

"Halt thou traveler... Do not dare enter this city if thou should not recall Water is the key of Heaven."

Nicholas was too excited. The submerged city in front of him seemed to have been surrounded by two large castle walls extending to both sides from the entrance gate. The walls were in ruins at some places. But the towers on the walls stood erect. The tower walls shed light. As he entered, he saw a large pyramid ahead which did not resemble the Egyptian structures. The top of the Alinapolis pyramids seemed to have a hexagonal top. He had counted about eight of these in the city. As he was curiously examining the sights among the ancient pleasant sounds of Alinapolis, he heard the Jug Carrier's voice:

"Those pyramid-like strange structures you see were living, health and energy centers of Alinapolis. These buildings contained within them water happily flowing from section to section in the forms of cool and hot liquid and steam. Special personnel whispered special words to the waters in the jugs on behalf of the patients, there were swimming pools. But most importantly the structures which forwarded the special water to the walls which shed light to the streets and houses..."

As the Old Man walked slowly to the other window, he continued his speech:

"A citizen of Alinapolis took a bath everyday... Cleanliness was their greatest ritual. They learned it from King Solomon... They relaxed under the steamy domes seated on horseshoe arches and washed themselves clean on hot circular marble blocks. These facilities in the building were open to all people's use at all times."

Nicholas thought he understood the purpose of those buildings. He concluded it, "in other words, the main mechanism which generated electricity". Nicholas pressed his face to the windows to see the furthest points of the city. Interestingly, the sea water was quite clear and there was visible no fish. Bubbles seemed to perk up from around the buildings resembling pyramids. The secrets revealed by the Old Man danced among the ancient sounds of Alinapolis:

"If Egyptian hieroglyphics are examined closely, one could see the technological vehicles such as aircrafts, helicopters and others including paintings of humans in flight. Their papyrus mentions flying men who brought death to their city... These were the Mu, the people from Alinapolis. They pictured the vehicles used by Alinapolis. King Solomon had taught to his senior aides the secrets of water which eventually led to advanced technologies not seen previously"

It seemed every window looked at different scenery. The houses were duplex mostly made of stone. Without exception, each had pools with fountains. Houses were built around the immense structures resembling pyramids. The Sage remained silent and did not interfere with Nicholas' curious peeks at the city. The marble walls between the windows were very strange. They seemed to alter their color from navy blue, blue, to black tones as one walked by. They were like plasma technology screens. He felt as if he watched himself as he passed. The Old Man's voice was very certain and required Nicholas' full attention:

"After a sovereignty of 700 years, the rulers of Alinapolis began using Water not for their own prosperity and happiness but as a weapon... They acquired machinery which could fly long distances and spread death to others. They used the power of Water for extreme violence. Consequently they acquired open and secret enemies. Violence begets violence... And, enemies never sleep... In a moment of blindness or oversight even the most powerful empire ends..."

They walked slowly by the windows while observing the submerged city. In front of a round window standing alone in the entire hall, there was a seat like a king's throne.. It was decorated and ornamented beautifully with mother of pearl engraved finely in the dark wood covered with carved motifs. The eagle with wings spread at the head of the seat was prominent. The table in front of the seat contained a visible pentagram similar to that of Solomon's seal was intriguing... And just opposite to the throne was the magnificent scenery of Alinapolis submerged in water and shedding brilliance from all of its walls…

As the Old Man sat on the throne he asked Nicholas to bring a chair. He grabbed one from the table nearby and thought "the chair is too beautiful to sit on. In Alinapolis they must have had a terrific life style". He placed the chair to the left of the Sage and sat down. As he was waiting for what was coming, the Old Man reached forward to the small table in front of him and pulled a drawer open. He gently removed a thick book with a very old leather cover. Like a ritual, he handed it to Nicholas in silence with piercing eyes fixed on his. Nicholas carefully accepted it with both hands and noticed that the title inscribed in embossed gold: THE LAW OF WATER. He slowly flipped open a page with great interest. It was a hand-scripted book. Pages were yellowish and the writings were in green. The Old Man simply said, "Close it now. You will examine it in America". Nicholas obeyed instantly and apologized. The Jug Carrier turned his eyes to Alinapolis visible from the big round window. He spoke in a sorrowful and distant voice which was a reflection of his tired gaze to the ancient city:

"They learned that water reacts to each word and converts into anything desired. They learned to achieve any alteration in their bodies through the use of water. This knowledge was given to them by King Solomon. They understood the value of water in God's presence. They discovered how music affected water. How evil words changed water. Most importantly, they understood that their bodies and organs were mostly water, and a mixture of salt and water flowed in their bodies. They sensed that a sea was inside them. Thus they discovered that words -kind or evil- altered their bodily fluid balance. When they eventually applied the full knowledge of water, they never knew any disease. Neither obesity nor any others… They reached the peaks of pleasure. They lived very long... They were in Heaven while on Earth... Alinapolis was the paradise on Earth..."

The Old Man stopped. The ancient sounds of Alinapolis filled the hall and Nicholas sat there silently in awe with an ages old hand-scripted book on his hands in a magnificent Palace room with windows looking at wondrous Alinapolis. He tried to comprehend all that transpired and all that he had heard. The citizens of Alinapolis had lived a wonderful life with the secrets of water. All their problems were resolved with the magic of water. This was so wonderful and elegant.

When the Old Man shut off the device capturing sounds from times long since gone, a silence settled in the palace hall. Nicholas came to his senses. He heard the pleasant voice of the Sage echoing:

"Water possesses immense powers. It is alive. It can merge with anything around it. It reflects the full character of anything it absorbs. It reacts to music and to words spoken directly. Never humiliate water. Its molecules modify their energy according to intent of words used. When water becomes dirty, it is simply because it has taken upon itself to purify something else... Nicholas, in reality, water never gets dirty... Water evaporates to the sky and returns to earth fully cleansed. The amount of water on this planet has always remained constant since the creation of Earth. Water has always been identical to the water that existed in the very beginning. So you must pay much respect to this ancient being which has always been here. Be very mindful of your words. It reacts to every single word uttered... "

Nicholas had been listening to the amazing explanations with great interest. He was shocked. What has been described about water he had been consuming without paying any attention or a single thought was incredible. The Old Man was still talking thoughtfully with his eyes locked on the submerged Alinapolis.

"Hearing nice words pleases humans. Same is also true for water. Just like humans, in fact more so, the water also reacts sensitively to all that transpires around it. While flowing in a furious waterfall, it is very happy and alive, but when chlorinated and flowing out of tap spout after passage through the pipes, it is unhappy and lifeless.. It responds positively to the words of love... negatively to the words of hatred…"

Leaving the window, the Sage walked slowly toward the throne seat after finishing what appeared to be his loud thinking... Sat on the throne and looked at Nicholas still standing by the window.

"The most important thing you should know is that water is alive."

Nicholas nodded obediently and very visibly to affirm his understanding of the instruction which sounded like a command and warning. The Old Man picked up the water jug he had left beside the throne a little while ago. Poured a little water to the cup which was attached to the jug at all times. He slowly and delicately placed the jug on the floor. Closed his eyes and began drinking with small sips. Nicholas was still in front of the window and took glimpses of the submerged city while being very careful not to appear ignoring the Old Man. But after a few moments of innocent neglect, he suddenly became aware of the Old Man's presence near him when he heard his voice again... As the Old Man joined Nicholas in gazing the city by standing near him, the words dropped from his lips one by one:

"Nicholas… Never forget this... The only secret of living healthy and long like them is… *Water*..."

Nicholas looked at the man in a way very suggestive of his desire to question after all that he had heard. But as the Old Man turned his eyes to the sight at the bottom of the sea standing beyond the window, Nicholas couldn't muster up any courage to say anything. They both remained silent for an extended period and looked at the scene ahead of them. Then unexpectedly the Sage pointed at something:

"Look... Apapol is still operating. It is still blowing the reconstituted water from its top. That is the reason for serene clear waters and absence of fish."

When Nicholas focused at the spot pointed out, he realized that it was one of the strange structures resembling Egyptian pyramids.

Nicholas mumbled in a whisper, "So... it is called Apapol." He tried to understand what "blowing reconstituted water" meant. He concluded that these strange buildings must be converting water in a special way in Alinapolis. When Nicholas moved a little closer to the window for a better peek through the deep sea water, he noticed that the Old Man walked decisively and suddenly back to the throne nearby... Once seated, he caught with his own the eyes of Nicholas observing him curiously:

"It is not possible not to wonder when confronted with the magnificent design of each water molecule... They have internal patterns like the rarest brilliants. Now your scientists are able to photograph these structures with advanced technology. You can research and see these beautiful crystalline patterns... But now, the water used by most people does not have these patterns.. In fact, the water is not even alive... "

The Old Man gestured at the ancient hand-scripted book he had handed over to Nicholas a little while ago.

"In that, Law of Water which I gave you, there are crystalline pattern drawings corresponding to the special words spoken... The book contains the alphabet of the water. Learn it well..."

Nicholas had already returned near the Old Man and had taken the seat near the throne. He was listening carefully listening to words spoken by the Man Carrying a Water Jug. Nicholas had been warned previously at a room of Hagia Sophia with the instruction; "you will write what I have told you" while receiving that ancient book and a special pen. He felt the responsibility of a duty assigned to him and he listened hard as if to memorize each word said. He was hard pressed to resist the temptation to flip open the Water Law book he was holding on devotedly. At the same time he was pondering the possibility of "Water having an alphabet... Could this be real?" Nicholas had returned to the questions he was unable to answer. This state of mind seemed to have become normal for him since his journey had begun...

The Old Man pulled the drawer of the small table in front him and took out what appeared to be a sizeable ornamented glass. Upon a more careful look, Nicholas noticed that the decorations were identical to the special glass pen given to him earlier. The Old Man poured a little water to the glass from his Jug. Left the jug and held the glass in his both hands. Focused his sight to the interior of the glass and, as if to the water inside, he began talking...

"Nicholas... remember... The unequalled patterns of the water molecules change with every word they hear... molecules transition from one pattern to another with each word...

Beautiful words such as "Thank you", "Love", "Gratitude", and "I love you" cause the molecules to obtain pattern motifs like those of fabulously crafted crystals with extremely refined lace. But evil words such as "I will kill you", "Damn you", or "You are driving me insane" do not cause formation of any patterns and the water does not crystallize. Do not forget... For these to happen, water must be alive... Lifeless water has no supreme benefit other then temporarily quenching biological thirst... And if you drink that lifeless water while standing up... it may even harm you.."

Nicholas was looking at the glass in amazement. Could such a thing be possible? The Old Man took a sip from the glass and added:

"Nicholas... Some of your scientists photographed with an electron microscope a water molecule which they offended by saying "you make me sick!!". They saw that the water exhibited a cell structure like that of cancer. Then, they told sweet soothing words to the offended and heart broken water... They observed that the water regained its beautiful original crystalline patterns. But it wasn't easy... It took days to heal the water to its original state"

Every time the Old Man uttered a word, a new secret was revealed. While Nicholas was busy with these thoughts, the Sage held the glass close to his lips, and instead of taking a sip, he gently whispered to it. Words which Nicholas couldn't hear... It appeared to be a silent sentence or two like a prayer. Then he closed his eyes and took several sips with distinct pauses in between. Turned his piercing eyes to attentive Nicholas. It was obvious that he had further instructions for him:

"...I told you about patterns corresponding to words spoken. To fully command water, to comply with your wishes, you must first reform its molecules to a perfect hexagonal array... This is only possible with special sentences spoken. Then, only then, water becomes your elixir... cure for all problems... Always remember… water must be alive in the first place… and you need special words and phrases…"

He placed the glass on the small table in front of him. Extended his hand and asked for the book. Nicholas quickly responded and respectfully handed over the Book. The Old Man randomly opened a page in the mid portion of the thick book. Flipped a few pages and said:

"Look… right here… Here are some pattern pictures corresponding to words spoken… These pictures show incredible reflections of water. Never forget… water is alive and must always remain alive to be useful… Water is a substance which reacts to all feelings and thoughts. It is affected instantly."

He returned the book to Nicholas with that page open. Then he opened the small table drawer again and took out another book which appeared like modern day photo albums. Handed it to Nicholas...

"See… These are the photographs I mentioned to you… Take a good look at both…"

Nicholas knew what to do when the Old Man became silent again. He perused in amazement the patterns of the ancient Book and the photographs taken by the latest technologies. He heard the Jug Carrier add:

"Leonardo Da Vinci drew the patterns in that scripted book. Don't sell this one, too…"

The Sage had said this affectionately in a teasing manner, but Nicholas couldn't stop himself from feeling embarrassed by the hint and lowered his head. He wanted to say something apologetic, but didn't think it would change anything. He tried to comprehend the timing of the hint and wondered if it might have a serious message he didn't grasp. Why did he say this now? The question on his mind was enough to demoralize him. But he pulled himself together and turned his full attention to the patterns sketched by Da Vinci. The molecular patterns corresponding to the phrases "I love you" and "Thank God" had beauty which would have made even the most talented jewellery designers jealous. On the other page were patterns reflected by water to the phrases such as "Damn you" and "I'll be sick anyway". These patterns were mixed, irregular and blurry without any crystals. On the pages there were also the names of what appeared to be cities or towns, and drawings of spring wells. He did not recognize most of the names. But the patterns were wonderful.

While Nicholas was absorbed in the beauty of the sketched patterns, he noticed that the Sage was rising from his throne. Nicholas acted quickly, left the books on his chair and immediately followed the Old Man. This time they were slowly walking in front of the right side windows of the palace hall.. At each brief window stop, the submerged city looked even more incredible... A strange indescribable joy and odd excitement had taken over him... Just as he was concentrating on the submerged images, the Old Man spoke softly:

"The divine powers of water causes information interchange among the cells. This is how we are able to exist. Everything which crosses your mind during any day and whatever you say affects all your cells at the same time. Because water in your body instantly absorbs and transmits these energies to your cells. Eventually you become what you think and what you say. In the meantime, your body alters. For example, Nicholas, when you say something negative like "I always get sick", this negative information will instantly change the character of your body fluids and transfer this character to the cells. Then you will suffer the consequences... Inevitable..."

He stopped suddenly. From this window it appeared that the palace they were in looked at Alinapolis from overhead. The entire city was in the valley below. He felt himself standing on a observatory. An Apopal nearby was blowing pressurized water from its hexagonal top. The Old Man was also absorbed in this majestic and mysterious underwater scenery. But he nevertheless spoke to his disciple with his gaze firmly fixed on the remnants of ages long gone:

"One can only live at the quality of one's thoughts and utterances. You are what you think and what you say. Your entire life and health is the coded information in your cells inherited from your blood line and your own past registered in your own body water. If you wish to change and become anew as a human first, you must alter the character of water in your body. Change the words you use and watch your life change. The water in your body and the living water you consume respectfully and lovingly will do it for you. Always keep in your mind that you can only exist at the quality level of your thoughts, your words and the water you consume..."

Nicholas understood this well. He gently redirected his eyes to the submerged ancient city standing naked in the valley below beneath the waters. He was juggling in his mind all that he had heard while looking at Alinapolis which seemed to have jumped out of a tale. The Apapol he was seeing from this side of the palace was different than those at the city entrance visible on the other side. This one had near it towering structures which looked like windmills. In the meantime he made sure to remain in glancing contact with the Old Man in anticipation of additional knowledge. The Sage had a cold gaze and appeared deeply engaged with the Apapol ahead of them. After a long silent observation of the ancient submerged quiet city, he left the window and walked along the hall. Nicholas followed while feeling part of a magical tale reflected in the wonderful ornamentations of the palace hall... The silence had continued unexpectedly long. Then the wise words of the Old Man requiring Nicholas' full attention continued:

"One's vibrational energy, thoughts, words, ideas, the music listened to, even the films and shows one watches alter the molecular character of water... Water is the source of life... Human body is like a sponge... It consists of trillions of cells like minute rooms formed mostly of fluids. The quality of life is directly connected and proportional to the quality of water in the body. Water is an extremely adaptable substance. Physically it adapts easily to its environment, but keep in mind that it also alters its molecular arrangement. The vibrational energy it receives from its surroundings affects the molecular structure. Spoken words are nothing more than vibrations. Human body consists of 85% water. Hence all thoughts and vibrations are absorbed. Thoughts and words determine the quality of one's life... In fact we form and create our lives with the words we speak which influence the constitution of water in our bodies..."

What Nicholas was hearing bewildered his soul and mind... It appeared that ideas such as "each determines their own fate" stated by some famed philosophers had been correct all along. Clearly, water in the body reacting and responding to words while constantly reforming the inner patterns made the quality of life highly dependent on thoughts and words used in daily life.

Nicholas had seen and heard this in a recent scientific research documentary. Yes... each word is a unique vibration without a doubt... Names are nothing, but unique vibrations... hearing one's name affects the person deeply with its vibrations.

And one's name ultimately determines one's fate...

Gently caressing the palace columns, Nicholas followed in deep thought while the Old Man's mysterious and subtlest sentences echoed:

"Water drunk either from a silver cup, earthen jug, or worse, from a plastic container is different, why? It is for the same reason why tea sipped from a hip endowed sensuous glass is different from a porcelain cup... Tea devotees make this strange distinction... Why is this variation in perception when the molecules are the same as stated by the science of chemistry?"

As if pondering the profound reason himself, the Sage's words came to an abrupt end. Short silence ensued. Judging the familiar pause, Nicholas intuitively knew that the question was not posed to him. He kept silent and waited in anticipation. The dramatic monologue which had firmly embraced Nicholas' mind and soul amidst palm-branched pillars of the palace hall... Facing the silent aquatic city appearing to have emerged from a tale of an ancient tragedy, the Sage began again:

"What causes distinct taste is the reaction of water to differing substances. Chemically, water is still the same, but somehow its character changes. Its vibration alters. Chemistry, originally known as *alchemy* in its motherlands to the East does not fully comprehend this subtle variation in character. Alchemy, now referred to as '*Quantum Physics*', hide the secrets. In some minor way it explains the taste difference.... Nicholas... Did I hear you say how?"

Smiling, the Old Man turned around and looked at Nicholas. For a moment Nicholas was terrified... Wondered if he had voiced a word or sound, or habitually mumbled something... To his greatest relief, he instantly realized that the Sage was again teasing him affectionately...

As if to alert Nicholas to the words which was to follow, the Old Man's voice reassumed its serious tone:

"..Water records information... As it does, it also gains new qualities. But its chemical structure does not change. Only its vibration becomes different... Chemistry is concerned with its molecular structure and elements... While quantum physics is more interested in its vibrational characteristics... Structure is the organization of molecules... Molecules form a group as clusters... These are the memory cells. What operates this memory system is the Water Alphabet... and one can create sentences with this alphabet or change the existing ones..."

They approached the opposing wall of the hall. Here, too, were rectangular windows as in other areas, but in contrast, only two... There was a magnificent large cartouche painting in between. As Nicholas was examining the artwork, he also expected intently further revelations of the mysterious alphabet. He had been informed of the presence of an alphabet when the Old Man handed over the hand-scripted ancient book, but he hadn't seen it yet. He was quite curious. He had previously seen news about a Japanese research company working on a technology which would imprint water. The company was able to form temporary images on water surface. But it seemed the Man Carrying a Water Jug was referring to a far more special case. As Nicholas contemplated these strange notions, the Old Man was preoccupied with the Alinapolis outside... At the window adjacent, his gazing eyes were at a distance and sorrowful. Turning at Nicholas, he added softly:

"Scientists claim the discovery of 440 thousand information nodes in each memory cluster cell. In reality, it is much more... Each node stores all the surrounding information. Each node interacts in a special way with its environment. During this interaction, water records its relationship with the world like a magnetic tape. Any change in its environment, even the slightest, the light in the room, your happiness or anger, your prayers, your gratitude... any conceivable thing... affects water and changes its internal state. Not only those... all realms... all dimensions... even the information in our dreams are recorded and stored...

Jesus' conversion of the sea to wine, Moses' partitioning of the sea into two halves, rain-prayers being answered with rain, baptizing, offering to water devotion in the far eastern lands and prayers followed with a breath puff, mantras, hymns, bodily cures by sound vibrations, giving thanks to nutrition which is essentially water, blossoming encouraged with music are the results of sentences carried in the memory of water... Nothing ever compares to the alphabet of water... Nicholas... you will see it in that book... Water is capable of anything with that alphabet... It becomes an enormous power... Sometimes quenching a thirst, sometimes a purifier, a comforter... and a cure... and sometimes a furious devastator of all which confront it... all due to its alphabet..."

Silence ensued... Like mantras revolving in his head, Nicholas kept repeating them silently as if to memorize every subtlety. The Old Man was once again drawn into the sight of Alinapolis. His sorrow was clearly visible... While Nicholas was trying to grasp the essence of spoken words and its association with the sorrow present in the palace air, the revelation as if a serial of intimate confessions by a master to his apprentice, pounded once again in Nicholas' over-stretched mind:

"Yes... Water has an alphabet... Never forget... God's supremely endless powers come through it... Coping of mortals become possible. God loves water.. It is a special creation... A medium for transfer of goodness and force... This is the reason why water's color, although present, not seen among all others, its taste not possible to include among the known, its aroma not classifiable or describable... *Knowest thou most heavenly water for it is purest gift of God...* This is why one must always cleanse oneself thoroughly to be closer to God. This is the basic rule for admittance into his realm... All negative vibrations are thus neutralized by cleansing. Else... Beware... none is immune to such neglect's future consequences. No obstacles must stand in your way......"

Appearing stressed, the Sage stopped abruptly... seemed to be regathering his thoughts... and then added only one sentence with a decisive and firmer voice tone, clearly intending the statement to be final:

"Let water befriend you... Do not deny... not for a moment... your loyalty to this heavenly power... Otherwise its secrets will permanently avoid you. Beware... Nicholas!"

This precise command, combined with the Old Man's piercing eyes was more than sufficient to prompt Nicholas, without a moment's delay, to affirm his full obedience with a sharp nod. But, rarely did the Man Carrying a Water Jug parted his eyes from the submerged scenery of Alinapolis. Ever since their entry to this palace hall, the Old Man's demeanor was strange indeed. Much different than that in above floors... He kept engrossing in the sight at dark bluish depths ahead and never neglected to touch his aged, surveying hands sadly to all that is around him...

After remaining silent for an extended period in front of the window, the Old Man slowly turned to Nicholas and approached him with lingering hesitant steps. Stopped next to him. Now they were both as if peering at a glamorous painting in an art gallery.

The cartouche artwork on the wall was beyond any mortal's imagination. An incomparable beauty and gracefully endowed female *aendahm* with a woven blonde bunned hair, leaning on her left shoulder, deep noble eyes and heavenly physique to challenge any frozen appetite and heart...

As Nicholas focused on the statuesque, wantonly daring beauty affixed to the wall, the references to women made above in Hagia Sophia by the old Man Carrying a Water Jug, took a sudden and clear form in his mind... Never was he ever so absolutely certain of the divinity and enamored by the beauty of God's feminine creation. He couldn't help but think over and over: "God has created all women with immeasurable heavenly magnificence..."

From the first moment onward, the beautiful female depicted so sensuously in the wall cartouche, merged mesmerizingly with the vivid and voluptuous mental images of Kristen...No primal sensation had ever conquered him so very completely. The thought of Kristen once again ruptured his heart. This strange feeling was not fathomable. It tore him apart...

The Jug Carrier standing near him was just as frozen.. The affectionate glitter in his eyes was noticeable. Nicholas did feel the longing, love and deep pain in those tired, reminiscing glitters. He wanted to enquire if this woman of depths might be the Princess Alina. But, did not venture... He no longer had any question privileges...

The Old Man stepped closer to the cartouche artwork. He touched figurine as if wanting not to disturb it. Stood there silently for an unexpected period as if paying long overdue devotion. Nicholas, while intently observing the sad composition in front of him, couldn't help but think also of the revelations just trusted to him. Too abruptly, the Old Man departed with quick steps. Nicholas chased right after him wondering, "...what happened now..?"

It was utterly surprising... That dominant saddened demeanor had dissipated in a moment's notice, and the Old Man was back again to his royal kingly ways... They crossed the hall briskly... ...and silently... When they reached the throne, the Old Sage signalled the nearby seat to Nicholas. When Nicholas sat down with utmost respect, there was a brief uneasy silence. Nicholas knew immediately that this was the typical silence to be followed with further mysterious explanations. It wasn't long before the Old Man began speaking again:

"Nicholas... the Water I've been talking about is not the ordinary water which you see around you... from taps... in bottles... I am talking about the *Living Water*... *Water* which has not been abused with chemicals, pollutants or pipes running around..."

Nicholas detected frustration in his voice. A mild anger perhaps... The Old Man's pursuant silence was very meaningful... purposeful... As Nicholas was trying to put this new and unusual situation in a perspective within his overburdened mind and soul, the Old Man once again reached at his earthen jug and gently took a little amount of water in the small cup which was never separated. Instead of sipping it in his customary old ways, he just kept looking into it as if observing a realm beyond... Nicholas awaited with intense curiosity. He had no idea what to anticipate. His perplexed mind was refocused with the words which accompanied:

"Water... the gentlest of all substances... looses all its vitality within 230 feet of piping due to the pressure it is subjected to... The pressure required for delivery of water to the houses also causes destruction of water's internal harmony and dynamism...

Water has a double helix spiral internal motion. This assists the formation of divine crystals within. When spirality is deformed, crystal is destructured and no geometry is possible... Thus... no information... no vitality... but... God's infinite power embedded in water permits reconstitution of the lost vitality... and returns water to life... Take that water and let it rest in an earthen jug at a quite part of your home. The earthen jug will readjust the geometry of water. Natural earth is a catalyst... The quality of earth used is very important. Nicholas... I'll show you a location where the soil is suited to the recovery of vitality in water. A jug made of it will reconstitute the lost structure of water. Actually, any earthen jug one can buy at an ordinary market will also do a good job. The water you get will be the closest in character to real Water I've been referring to all along. And this water will actualize any wish concerning your physical being..."

He turned and looked with a smile at Nicholas... And quickly added:

"...by the way... you'll never know... perhaps the angels of inspiration will visit you and whisper their offers of fresh bright ideas... you might even become rich like a Mogul..."

As silence settled once again, the Old Man preferred a mischievous grin... an indication of his good natured one sided jostling... Nevertheless, Nicholas couldn't help but wonder the true nature of these last few affectionate and teasing words... They bore sharp hints, seemed unusually dislocated and were unexpectedly removed from the seemingly natural course which the Old Man's monologue had been following all along. The reference to "...angels of inspiration..... bright ideas..." had suddenly numbed Nicholas and struck him with yet another new question on the potential relationship of 'inspiring angels' with living water... What could it possibly be... and how?

Unexpectedly, the Man Carrying a Water Jug arose and walked to the round window nearby. He was still wearing on his face that innocent, affectionate but hinting sly grin. Nicholas knew instinctively that the Old Man was preparing a new surprise. Like an ancient silhouette misplaced in time, he firmly stood facing the window. As if to explain his longevity defying the ages bygone, the wise Old Man devotedly holding his companion the earthen jug and gazing through the round window into the depths ahead of him, simply said:

"Long and healthy life is a function of mass and weight... The only thing which will ensure longevity and endurance is the Living Water and its sipping method... Both go hand in hand like everlasting love..."

Nicholas did feel that he was now able to grasp the subtle and underlying meanings of all he had heard... It seemed he indeed had traversed an entirely new dimension in search of the truth... It seemed the Old Man's words did radiate the primordial and profound secret of this Planet... Nicholas knew he shouldn't remain seated. "Being seated" he felt would be far too "disrespectful to the Sage" who generously provided such enormous and wise guidance... He quickly stood and rushed to the round window to join his mentor who at that moment had already begun speaking:

"Take Living Water from Nature.... Preserve it only in earthen jugs... Keep the jugs in a peaceful and silent environment... for 7 days... and each dawn, noon and sunset, repeat three times your innocent but realistic wishes... no sense and logic in demanding billions or flights of fancy... wish for good health and love for all... wish preservation from human frailties... ask for a shield against arrogance and conceit... ask for general good health... tell Kristen to ask for sustenance of her delightful beauty... But... none should ever neglect 'respect and love' for Living Water... One's heart's purity is instantly reflected with highest sincerity in Water... It shouldn't be so difficult to confess love of God through Living Water which at all times is in the realm of Divine. It shouldn't be too difficult to say 'I Love You'... At least three times a day... From dawn to sunset... Then, after the sunset on the seventh day... Sip the Living Water gently at intervals... in the exact way you were instructed... Close your eyes... Fear not... Be pure and sincere in thought... as you stand eyes closed... courageously and lovingly... on the threshold.... predawn of God intended dimensions and bright paths allotted to you in this Cosmos... Remember and rest assured in the divine powers of Living Water... Never forget that Water has long memory if not abused... disturbed... offended or dishonored... The information is in there... all of it... without any exceptions... Never forget water's immense capacity to record information... and never forget that *What thou shall sow...So shall thou reap... So shall it be written... So shall it be done...* Never forget these words.. Nicholas... my son..."

Nicholas was suddenly elated beyond his comprehension. He fell deep into a swelling and swirling well of love for the Old Man who had just referred to him as "my son". He trembled with delight of such a privilege... He wanted to scream his joy... but confined himself to mature stance of loyalty and devotion... Eyes fixated on Alinapolis in front of the circular window, the Man Carrying a Water Jug clearly had not yet finished his words of immeasurable wisdom:

"...naturally, cure of ailments are all there in Living Water... for some water loved for seven days... for some forty days... but always living water from therapeutic springs everywhere on this Planet... Beware... the cure is there..."

When the Old Man turned to Nicholas, it was self-evident that another journey was about to end… Speaking with intermittently paused precise words, he said to Nicholas:

"Even the insane or the unfortunate precious children with defects of cognition can be cured… Do not be fretful… Holier and much deeper knowledge of cures by Living Water shall be fully revealed to you…"

The Old Man turned at proud Alinapolis silently patient beneath the waters of the Bosphorus… Pointing at the Apopal ahead he said:

"You perceived those only as means which convert water into energy… True… But the Apapols were also known as *Aquacade Clinics* or *Aquatic Hospitals* among the citizens of Alinapolis… These were centers of health, happiness and longevity… places where all evils of highly vulnerable spirits and bodily diseases were cured… with special Living Water… This ancient knowledge was revealed many centuries later to a special one among the Ottomans… who in turn pioneered spreading of this vital information in the Empire from here in Istanbul… Living Water Cure Centers were established everywhere from this Capital of the Empire onward to all the provincial centers like Edirne and Bursa… Historical records of cures for countless diseases exist… even cures for insanity are documented…"

Appearing to prefer silence, the aged Sage halted his knowledge-filled wondrous speech. His frail fingers locked in hands behind and just two steps removed from the hall window, the Old Man stood there looking at the deep blue hazed, not too distant aquatic city laying in the depths of ages gone. While standing near him at a respectable distance, Nicholas' guts were churning in excitement of mystique which had enveloped his soul. Nicholas did appear to be sharing the insanely beautiful sight which stood in front of them, but he did not neglect observing his wise teacher with frequent hesitant glimpses taken from the side. At the same time his mind was storming with teachings he had been receiving, particularly by those he had just been given. He tried to fathom the incredible dimensions of it all. Perhaps this was the main secret of the world. Did the Old Man not say that Alexander and Genghis Khan had marched non-stop with their armies in pursuit of the secret of immortality? Nicholas clearly recalled the Old Man's words spoken while they were seated at the edge of Hagia Sophia dome: "…I too was a powerful ruler and commander like them…" Could it be that this man had already reached that secret?

As Nicholas was struggling with these strange but powerful questions, he was startled by the unexpected voice of the Sage:

"Becoming rich is not linked purely to luck… Dreams do not make you rich! Dreaming immeasurable wealth in expectation of a heavenly grant approval from a finite and terminal cosmos is nothing but foolish to say the least... In our perceptions… Cosmos appears as an infinite, magnificently tremendous and unfathomably abundant creation of God... but... nevertheless... It still is a creation with limitations and an end... *Thou shalt not ask that which cannot be rightfully granted...* In the subtleties of these heavenly words... Nicholas... hidden are the universal fairness and limitations… Nevertheless... becoming wealthy could be the result of a momentary idea conceived... Naturally great efforts must follow... but a beautiful idea conceived is the prerequisite... *Water* is the most magnificent preserver of knowledge. Information for every moment of the past, present and future is stored in the water... God's powers are inexplicable... words will never suffice. As God's powers traverse water… much residue of this force remains in it… Thus... most precious notions and knowledge are stored in water. Wealth of all types do come with just and correct thoughts... Profound and good ideas are fundamental... and water possesses the unimaginable ideas of all dimensions...

Where do you think the inspirations for the poet or musician originate?.. What one might call the *angel or fairy* of inspiration is nothing but the sudden emergence in one's mind of knowledge stored within water... How else could one explain mind-boggling discoveries of scientists? If one consumes living water... if one has a healthy mind and body... a gentle soul no doubt... then the hidden knowledge stored in water will whisper unto you... thus comes to you the magical inspiration to be resolved at long last..."

Perplexed with the incredible impact of mind and soul whirling words heard, Nicholas just stood there looking at the Alinapolis deep outside... He looked indeed but was unable to pierce through the mesmerizing combination of intense feelings, teachings and the secretive mystique which cuddled him tightly... He felt extremely secure, at ease and in peace as if he had been raised to a higher level consciousness... The last points made by the Old Man were particularly striking and unbelievably enlightening... Nicholas couldn't help but conclude "so... when one says '..got an inspiration...got an incredible idea'... that is the moment in which what was stored in water surfaced at the brain... all source of inspiration therefore was the living water. One only had to supply a healthy and daily washed body, and purified soul. This could be had by drinking copius amounts of unhindered, unoffended and undisturbed living water..." Nicholas was ardent reader of books which told the stories of inventors and their discoveries since his high-school years... They all had one common question: "Why not?"

Yes... They all asked this question to themselves. As they recounted their experiences, the common thread was "... suddenly I thought of it... then I asked myself... Why not!"

Nicholas felt he was near a resolution. Ideas seemed to arrive unannounced and suddenly... and they began working on it... Clearly it was as if someone had whispered it to their minds. It was the living water whispering.

Nicholas was jerked out of his thoughts the moment he realized that the Old Man made a move to walk away from the window. Nicholas stood still few moments more observing the Old Man walking slowly and in deep thought toward the throne in the center of the palace hall. Nicholas headed hastily in the same direction as the Old Man sat on the throne. It wasn't long before the adorable voice filled with unending wisdom echoed in the hall:

"Take the book I gave you... We must now go upstairs"

Realizing these were the last moments in this mythical and mysterious place, Nicholas quickly turned his head toward Alinapolis for a final look. He could have stayed there endlessly and absorb the surrounding beauty of the city in aqua. With sadness and strange emotions he took one more look and surrendered to fate. Took the ancient, hand-scripted "Law of Water" book which had been sitting on the table and dashed after the Old Man. Touching the cool, smooth palace columns one by one as if to say goodbye, he caught up with his master who for a moment or two had stood at the palace hall entrance waiting for Nicholas.

They began their climb up in Hagia Sophia's deep secrets. Not an easy venture to climb up all those stairs which were not too challenging at the time when they travelled below. The Man Carrying Water Jug did stop for a brief rest on numerous occasions during their climb, and lectured Nicholas with his mysterious teachings. Nicholas was young and excited. He did not feel excessively the extreme difficulty of those endless steps going up.

He was further amazed with additional knowledge trusted to him on the way up by the Old Man.

Upon arrival at the section filled with ancient books the Old Man turned instead into the tunnel which Nicholas hadn't noticed during their way down only a while ago. As if to reassure Nicholas, the Old Man explained: "it is fairly late now… Tourists must be arriving… We shouldn't be seen. We must route from here to a different section."

They walked together through a narrow, seaweed and mold aroma cavernous passage. They stopped at a place appearing to be the end of tunnel. When the Old Man pushed gently the stone wall forward, they stepped out to the front of the small room off the garden in which they started their adventure some hours ago. This was the room where Nicholas was given that peculiar pen and the book which resembled the one he had unearthed in Jerusalem.

Visibly tired, the Old Man took a seat adjacent to the table at center of the room. Nicholas too felt the exhaustion of the night but did stand obediently near him. When the Old Man reached out his hand gesturing the book in Nicholas' hand, he respectfully leaned forward and handed the book over. Old Man flipped a few pages back and forth in final sections of the book. Having found what he was looking for the Old Man placed the open book on the table. Nicholas could easily see the odd, side by side figures on the pages. Nicholas looked silently and carefully. Expecting some type of explanation, Nicholas turned his eyes beggingly to the Old Man who replied instantly and stopped:

"Water's Alphabet!"

Once again, amazed, Nicholas reconcentrated on the pages containing odd but pleasant drawings. Some patterns resembled the punctuation *comma* which everybody knows. With an indescribable urge he felt the need to know how many figures there were... How many patterns did the alphabet contain? Curious, he counted carefully as he examined the page visually. Counted silently: 27 exactly...

Arrogantly, Nicholas teased himself: "I would have been surprised had it been any other number". As he was absorbed in the alphabet, he noticed the Old Man pull out a paper from the table's small drawer.

"Nicholas... in this scheme you will find the operational principles of a computer which works with water. When this computer is actualized the whole world will change irrevocably. This technology will open the gateways to unimagined new technologies... your level of technology currently uses only the binary system of 1s and 0s... But here there is an alphabet... Not the ordinary alphabets you are familiar with... This is *Water's* Alphabet... When the new computer operates on this basis... a remarkable, incredible, an unequalled new era of technology will commence on this planet. Well... here it is... From now on compose sentences from *Water*...."

During the following silence, perplexed Nicholas looked at the schema and the alphabet pondering "how the hell am I gonna build this computer?"

The Old Man arose... Approached Nicholas and grabbed him from the shoulders in a warm and fatherly manner...

"Write all that you have seen and what you've heard from me... Create a book... Read it once. Take your time... Later read it once again... but this time only the words which I've spoken... Thus you shall see the secret..."

Nicholas was not hesitant or reluctant, not for a moment, when committingly he replied in great devotion and respect:

"I shall do exactly as instructed... Sir... Please be assured that I shall take pride and joy in doing so".

Seemingly satisfied the Old Man gently turned away and slowly approached the side window of the room... It was a quite small window. Stood close right in front of it. He did appear studying the sight of morning at Hagia Sophia... In a very considerate and affectionate tone of voice the Old Man reiterated a question which has been among the heaviest in Nicholas' mind over the years. Especially since an invisible hand guided him from his home onward and landed him in Istanbul, he kept asking this question to himself frequently in fear...

The Sage, as if had been hearing these tribulations all along, simply said to Nicholas as he stood by the window..."You must be asking yourself again... What is all of this..? Why have these been happening to me? Why me?"

Clearly he wasn't expecting any replies... this was far too self-evident when he continued speaking without a glimpse at Nicholas...

"Recall your prayers offered while sick and gazing at the stars as a child in your Jacksonville home room... Recall your prayers given while lying under the stars at your home roof top. You've always looked at that occasionally glittering light in the night sky thinking it was the star light. You had noticed the intermittent glitters. You did make an extraordinary effort and waited hours on end for the next glitter. Fate unfolds in mysterious ways... All have been preordained... the only unknown has always been... who will assume the role and duty.... It is necessary to be fully prepared for the times when God spreads responsibilities... You... Nicholas... you... at this very moment... are in the very midst of your prayer granted... You were ready... You are among the *Chosen* indeed... You too are a *Carrier*..."

Nicholas was shocked. His heart tore the pieces in anxiety as the implications of the words *chosen* and *carrier* sank in the depths of his soul... Fearfully he kept murmuring in intense amazement. *"Chosen? ... Am I also a Carrier?"*

The Old Man, pretending not to hear the murmured questions, moved away from the window and slowly paced his way to the door. Opened it with a key from his pocket... When the squeaking door opened fully, the Old Man turned to Nicholas:

"Go immediately to your hotel..Gather your things at once..Take the first flight out... Go home to America"

These were strict and serious commandments. He pointed at the Water Law book which Nicholas was firmly holding on and said:

"Do as this book instructs... Live as indicated... Comply with every word inscribed... Conform fully to the guidance provided. Eat and drink according to the rules given unto you... always remember... *so it was written so shall it must be done...* When the time and place is right... we shall meet again... Do your utmost to solve the secrets... Never forget Nicholas... You are a Carrier! "

Night's exhaustion was still on him when he opened his eyes to the sound of his telephone. But, the excitement and joy he had during the night had not diminished. Eyes half asleep he sat up in his bed trying to focus on the phone screen. Just two cryptic words from Kristen read:

"Luvv u…"

With a plain family ceremony, Amber and Michael were engaged that night. Life was strange indeed. The interesting coincidence of meeting Amber and Kristen at Hagia Sophia continued after Nicholas had returned to New York. They met frequently. The friendship of Amber and Michael which began in New York had unexpectedly turned into a love affair. It was quickly and joyfully moving toward a potential matrimony.

At long last Nicholas had been able to say "Kristen…I love you" at the end of a romantic night. Those sweet feelings which flew from eyes to his heart had been wrapped in words and fell of his lips. Both were intoxicated in the vortex of a great love. During the moments they shared it seemed their spirits became aloft like the birds. This night was one of those moments. They had danced all night long and whispered love to each other's ears.

Nicholas feeling deeply satisfied responded happily to the warm love message on the screen:

"I love you too, my angel"

After sending the message he quickly headed to the bathroom. He had to rush to deliver on his promise to Kristen for a breakfast at Central Park. Under the shower he thought of the Man Carrying Water Jug who insisted on a clean and fresh start each and every day. It was nearly seven months since he had left behind those mysterious nights at Hagia Sophia. During this period he had gone through incredible changes because of the teachings and secrets given to him by the Man Carrying Water Jug. He applied all he had learned, especially the technique of drinking water. He stepped out of the shower. Felt he was rejuvenated with the energy and dynamism needed for a new day. He quickly walked to his dressing room in his new and spacious home. Stood motionless facing the full size mirror and smiled mischievously.

Within few days of his return from Istanbul, Nicholas had given to Michael the Da Vinci's 'Book of Secrets' he dug out in Jerusalem. He followed the advice of the Old Sage to the letter and Michael was tasked with sale of the ancient book. He recalled the day long intense stress he went through when courageous Michael dashed out for negotiations. His smile now on the mirror was a reflection of the fearful days which followed the sale. The memories of fear and suspicion on the streets, at home and the paranoia of being followed… The delusions of imminent harm at every corner and ring at the door… But at the end he had become wealthy and owned a luxurious penthouse in Manhattan. He continued to smile at the mirror and adapted a phrase from a world famous children's tale: "O mirror mirror on the wall... who is the smartest of them all?"

The new respect he acquired for water and drinking it in the manner prescribed by the Man Carrying a Water Jug had changed his attitude to life around him. He was overflowing with creative ideas. It was as if the clever fairies of inspiration were sitting on his shoulders at all times. A technology company was seriously interested in his idea of ultra-high frequency reduction by means of pure water contained in cellular baked clay. His internet photograph sharing site was booming. He had succeeded in cooking the sesame oil sweet the Old Man offered to him at Hagia Sophia. He even made plans for marketing of this health supplement. Moreover, he was about to finish the book in which he is accounting the details of his journey.

As he was putting on his shirt he admired the new smiling and energetic Nicholas in the mirror. He thought this good form and joy was the result of prescriptions given by the Man Carrying a Water Jug. The special clay jug he brought from Istanbul was stored at a quite corner of his new house. It was a new and secret ritual for him. He had not mentioned it even to closest buddy Michael but kept drinking from it every morning as he started his day. Now he better understood a sentence which he had heard as a child in a documentary:

"The unimpressive earthen jugs found in the most prominent location of the treasure filled tombs of the Egyptian pharaohs are a strange mystery..."

Nicholas now understood full well that this must be related to the knowledge imparted to him by the Old Man. He was certain that simple earthen jugs containing pure life giving water must have been placed prominently because they were the most precious items on the journey to beyond... Life giving pure water in simple jugs... the most important treasure of the pharaohs... not the golden accessories as most believe...

While still in his luxurious dressing room in front of the mirror, Nicholas recalled the words of the Old Man in Hagia Sophia:

"... the phrase.. *Opening Pandora's Box*... Actually there never was a *box*.. There was only an ordinary earthen jug. Erasmus of your so called *Renaissance* in Europe made a translation error... He confused the Greek word *pithos* with *pyxis* and it ended up being *Pandora's Box*... It should have been *Pandora's Jug*... Investigate this and you will find many things...

Mythology is persistent legends embodying some truths... often disguised as fantasies... If you dig into those you will encounter many messages which survived ages long gone... only incomprehension creates the unknown... what reveals the mystery is impatience enhanced with tolerant comprehension..."

The Old Man had suddenly reached for a water jug among the three on the floor. He had offered it to Nicholas with an affectionate smile. Seven months later Nicholas recalled vividly those sharp but loving eyes of the Old Man. Now it was so absolutely clear to Nicholas that the earthen jug given to him on that morning was in fact an incredibly great gift without any accompanying words. Nicholas appreciated now the whole episode so very absolutely and emotionally as he reviewed in his mind the last few sentences he had heard from the smiling Sage in Hagia Sophia:

"The only secret of healthy and long life is *living water*.. Nicholas...This jug I give you now shall forever remain with you. It is of earth from a holy place where our Madonna was instructed to live. I shall show that place to you in the future... Be patient... and wise... Now... Go back to your lands... Let this jug I've given befriend you... Soon you will see its mysterious miracles upon your life... Wait and see what the fairies of inspiration bestow upon you..."

The ringing phone jolted him.. He had almost finished dressing up. He quickly rose up leaving one shoe untied.. It was Michael.. Nicholas wanting to share his excellent morning mood with Michael joked in a jolly good fellow manner as he answered: "Ma'groom maan! You've been dreamin' of me, haven't you?" But, the unexpected response he got was shocking:

"Quick... Look at the newspapers... This Turk of ours committed suicide!"

"What suicide? Which Turk?"

Michael was clearly in fear and very concerned...

"Hell, Niko! Who else? Ali... the director of the auction house...the guy who bought the book.."

Nicholas panicked.. Dashed to his computer in the study room and clicked his favorite newspaper. Sure enough... It was on the headlines...

"Famed director of the Nobulstar Auction House, Ali Ertuğrul, is thought to have jumped off his 27th floor residence in Manhattan. The news of his death shocked the art world. Upon learning of the Facebook note 'Rest in Peace' left behind shortly prior by Ali Ertuğrul instigated an investigation by the New York Police Department".

Michael was still talking on the phone in a very concerned manner:

"Do you think this is what your Water Jug Carrier has forewarned? Why should a successful and happy, healthy man commit suicide? Why would anyone for God's sake? This smells fishy to me pal."

Michael's voice was filled with stress and worry... Nicholas thought to soothe him but he too was beside himself. Panic and fear had set in immediately. While he kept Michael on the phone he quickly read the news on another paper claiming that none of Ali's closest friends who can be reached had believed in existence of any reason why he should end his life. Ali's family was adamant...They were claiming that Ali could not have possibly done this.

Nicholas asked Michael to meet him and Kristen at the breakfast right away. He told him that he was on his way right now. He did not neglect to caution Michael to be extremely careful and be weary of the slightest suspicion. After Nicholas hung up and as he was tying his shoe-lace his mind was stuck on the number 27... the ever so present memory of the 03:27 did suggest a dreadful link... Fully ready, he rose quickly to leave home at once. Just one final glance at his computer screen really startled and froze him on the spot. The sliding news headline on the screen read:

"...Leonardo Da Vinci's Mona Lisa has been projected on the Moon with the latest laser technology..."

THE MAN CARRYING A WATER JUG SAYS:

"REJUVENATE YOURSELVES WITH WATER'S THOUSAND AND ONE MIRACLES"

*Softens the skin and reduces signs of aging.

*Brightens and enlivens the eyes.

*Eliminates exhaustion and provides youthful energy.

*Dehydration prevents production of sexuality hormones and causes impotence.

*Best way to lose weight is drinking water. Drink water as I prescribed. When you are hungry, do not overeat, and drink water frequently before you become thirsty.

*It reduces addictions of caffeine, alcohol and some drugs.

*It boosts immunity in cancerous and infected body areas.

*It slows loss of memory due to old age. Reduces the risks of Alzheimer's, Multiple Sclerosis, Parkinson's and Lou Gehring's diseases.

*Reduces stress, tension and depression.

*Protects against heart attack and paralysis.

*Prevents clotting in heart and brain vessels.

*Integrates mental and body functions. Improves decision-making and clear objective setting.

*Dilutes the blood and prevents cardiovascular clotting.

*Reduces menstrual pain and female heat flushes.

*Reduces pregnancy morning sickness.

*Human body does not have a specific organ as water reservoir. Regular day long water consumption is necessary.

*Regulates sleep.

*Protects against glaucoma.

*Regulates blood cell production in bone marrow. Reduces leukemia and lymphoma formation.

*Reduces the attention span problems in children and adults.

*Improves work productivity.

*It is drink which can be obtained easily and has no side effects.

*Provides energy for all brain functions

*It is necessary for the production of serotonin and other neural synaptic hormones.

*Necessary for all brain hormones including melatonin production.

*Best lubricant for digestive system and prevents constipation.

*Necessary for the regulation of body temperature.

*Purifies body by transporting toxins to liver and kidneys for discharge.

*Basic lubricant for the joints. Reduces arthritis and back pains.

*Strengthens vertebrae disks as shock absorbers.

*Deposits energy in food and energy is later transferred to human body.

*Dry foods must be avoided. Prefer food with liquids.

*Enables nutrient absorption and ensures distribution within the body.

*Improves efficiency of oxygen absorbing lung cells.

*Cells are oxygenated by water. Carries disposable gasses to the lungs.

*Prevents DNA damage and improves healing mechanisms.

*Improves immunity of bone marrow system.

*Basic solvent for vitamins and minerals, functions in the final metabolic stages.

*Assists cell electrical and magnetic functions, provides life force.

*It combines the internal substances in a cell.

*If water is consumed regularly day long, it will be easier to discern hunger from thirst.

*Dehydration causes deposits in most parts of the body, water dissolves and cleans these irregularities.

***Drink water while sitting as instructed. Water taken while standing travels quickly to the intestines. Sitting temporarily holds water in the stomach. This holding bay disinfects water with stomach acids and protects from any bacterial or microbic activity. Therefore, drinking water while seated and drinking it slowly a sip at a time with breathing in between sips helps protect human body from various infections including cholera.

www.ingramcontent.com/pod-product-compliance
Lightning Source LLC
Chambersburg PA
CBHW070529090426
42735CB00013B/2923